by Sylvia Ashton-Warner

MYSELF

by

Sylvia Ashton-Warner

Simon and Schuster · *New York*

To a Young Teacher

My dear:

Far too good an opportunity to overlook, replying to you between the covers of a book. Thank you very much for your letters. I like articulate people who know what they think and how to say it. You may even get as far as New Zealand some day to say in person what you think, over coffee or in the sun. Some Americans see the Pacific as no more than a paddling pool when it comes to getting where they want to; just pick up their skirts and wade across.

You are young and I like young company, from the cradle up. I've liked your letters over the years since I wrote *Spinster* and *Teacher*. You remind me how to listen again, an art overlooked when I was young. We all talk at once when we are young, isn't that so? We all know everything about anything at all . . . we are certain of it! Everything except correction. For one thing, talking flat out, we don't hear anyway, and for another we haven't got time to hear and if we should hear accidentally we don't agree with a word. Which from your end may sound pretty bad but from my end looks irresistible.

An exclusive art, listening . . . if I may digress so early in a letter. Until my late thirties I don't think it occurred to me to listen to anyone much and then only because I had to. Working on the Key Vocabulary I found that unless I listened, heard clearly, understood and felt what the children were saying I couldn't do what I wanted, whereas I'm a great one to do what I want if possible, even more so when impossible. An expensive exercise that, learning to listen, but worth it: expensive in patience but worth it in interest. Since then I've listened to everyone within earshot, to the five small children in this house including the new baby who says a lot and often. Without that discipline of listening to children during the Key Vocabulary I could have been deaf still; might not have been answering your letters but talking to myself.

Which brings me to the astonishing thing in your letters: you appear to have heard what I said. Being the reason I send this old manuscript along because *I* heard what *you* said. Wistful business, isn't it? this casual dialogue between mutually unintelligible generations like a separated seminar; letters jetting over continents and crossing oceans and far forgotten years.

I've been surprised at the humility in your letters. Not that humility does not make an excellent foundation on which to build a philosophy, a sound pad from which to blast off into unknown spaces; to equip yourselves for Operation Life humility could be the best storehouse of all. But my reaction has been that there could be more pride about, not only as an ambassador of your profession but in simply representing youth. "The widespread pride of man," from Whitman.

Of course I might be wrong. Pride might be there all the time but blurred by awe of me, yet I doubt if I'm awe material. I'm quite tame—at least I am now. I'm not saying I haven't picked up a few things that you have not been able to, being ahead of you along the road, but that doesn't make me awesome. If you saw me in the garden in my old clothes . . . if you saw me at my table in something loose, my writing table or if you heard me crooning to this new baby, my daughter's, you'd forget about the awe. Actually I find I know less as I go along this part of the track, and that others, know much more. In fact there are many senior teachers in other countries as well as in my own, from New York to Bangkok, London to Buenos Aires, to the west coast of Africa, who are better than I ever was, and it will do you good, at least clean up the awe, to read just what I was like when young—the original of *Teacher*. Not marvelous at all . . . frightful!

In this manuscript I admit much I don't like admitting, that I was anything but an example. Not a good teacher, not much of a person and a dead loss as a listener. I'm even risking my reputation by recording that I was not above loving with passion in forbidden directions, in several places at once, though honorably within the vows of marriage: on paper it looks selfish, but love was my big trouble when I was young —still is, to be frank; I should say love to me is still big but no longer trouble. My need of and dependence on it. I couldn't breathe without love in the air. I'd choke. I ceased to exist when not in love. The radiance within blotted out so that nothing would happen inside, nothing exploded into action. I can quite truthfully say that I never lifted a hand unless *for* someone: never took up a brush or a pen, a sheet of music or a spade, never pursued a thought without the motivation of trying to make someone love me.

But the hardest of all to expose to you is the violence that was in my character ever lapping and threatening near the surface, showing up in my nightmares. I could manufacture multitudes of magnificent and convincing excuses but excuses are boring, take too much time and use up too much paper.

For all that, I'm sending it along to—what I'm sending it for really is to—let me see . . . I'd like to say it is wholly a manner of answering all you have written to me, not from the wisdom of seniority which is not quite fair but from the stance of youth, putting you and me for once on the same age level, supplying a medium of comparison that is fair between us. Actually, I doubt that these revelations will help you as a teacher —nothing new professionally in them but insofar as there is inspiration from talking things over youth to youth confessing our mad mistakes, pontifically advising each other, lecturing each other on what we think and what the other should do, you may be supported as a young person possibly, as I would have been at that time. That's what I'd like to say and get away with it, but I suspect that is not the whole reason, nor the main one. The real reason lies elsewhere: as in everything I do, even in this, I want to win your indulgence and a smile for that person over twenty years ago. Not for the middle-aged me that I am but for that young person. That's what she wanted so terribly then. It's not too late.

Not that I assume for one moment that you are as confused as I was then, personally or professionally, but whatever our differences, however opposed our ways of seeing things, of going about doing a thing, there do remain codes in youth by which we understand each other, and it is in this area of the common hells and heavens of young people living it out, of young people trying to chart a course through the arduous terrain ahead; through the gullies, over the mountains and across the bleak plateaus, noting the voluptuous error of side-tracking glades and dells . . . it is on this blindfold track of blindfold decisions that it will give you something, this written memory, even if that something is only my own young company. At least you will know the language of the place.

I did however just in time get hold of one truth on my own when trying to plot my route: that not just part of us becomes a teacher. It engages the whole self—the woman or man, wife or husband, mother or father, the lover, scholar or artist in you as well as the teacher earning money so that a worthwhile teacher is one of the blooms from the worthwhile person, even though in my twenties and thirties I could neither isolate the different facets of the person nor balance them. They overlapped, merged and affected each other, infected each other often, with teaching itself the sounding board. If I was unhappy the schoolroom paid, if happy the schoolroom won. If I thought my husband wasn't pleased with me I didn't teach in tune but if he had kissed me before school in the morning I did teach in tune. When my own children were well the class was well but if one was sick I'd leave and go home. If I'd had time for early morning study I'd understand what I was doing but if I hadn't I wouldn't. Even what a lover said yesterday qualified the tone of the room and my finding out of all this was what sent me so deeply into study of myself and of the whole human self in order to try to become, not specifically a worthwhile teacher, but a worthwhile person first.

All that study I did on my own for years in isolation, that fierce attack on books. From those distant pages my youth thrusts questions: Do you study much? Do you passionately examine yourself, ruthlessly analyze yourself, do you agonize as I did between feeling and reason? Do you know the need to sit in silence over a thing, to follow a line of thought to a firm conclusion, then write down that conclusion? Do you retreat into solitude and consult your instinct when logic leaves you high and dry? Are you as confused as I was then, are you as bad as I was, as selfish, as foolish? I'd feel better about it if you are.

Do you too aim to be a worthwhile person or only a worthwhile teacher? How do you see teaching—as a source of income or as a work of global status? I wonder if you'll think, when you read through this, that I was moving in the right direction, if indeed I moved at all, or in the wrong direction— if you will think as I did then that war and peace might . . . only might . . . be in our hands, conceived in the early years of children, the classroom the incubator. Or will you think I was wrong?

· · ·

So here is this long letter of over two hundred pages in answer to all of yours. As a book it is unsound artistically on account of the balance disturbed by loving. Saul runs away with this story of a school; I know it and I could rectify it but I'll leave it because that's how it *was*. I could prune the references to him, in the interests of art, but it would no longer be how it was, for just as Saul unbalances this book so did my love for him unbalance my life when teaching on the River as possibly . . . even probably . . . a love in your own life at this moment disturbs your teaching. Besides, his inclusion is justified; our upsetting love enriched me as a person and therefore enriched the teacher.

Are you going to "go off" her—that young person—on account of her behavior: demanding from one man, running to the other? Please do not. Observe, yes, that she appears on paper selfish and willful, but understand and be faithful to her, allow for her vagaries, for if you in your youth do not, who will? Who knows—observed from the outside, confessed on paper, you may be as bad yourself? But Saul remains a gamble.

.   .   .

At my table looking out the windows I wonder what to say to you . . . to a young teacher. Across the spring garden, above the cineraria, through the trunks of the towering trees; over the silk water of the inner harbor I see the ships' entrance, beyond which is the tall Pacific and beyond that, your country. Only to find I have no advice.

I look back on fifty years, you look forward on fifty years. This world is yours, not mine. It was mine when I was young and I strongly knew it. True, there's a war on now but there was one on then; the world still belongs to you. For ever the world belongs to youth. Do you also strongly know it?

From fifty I have no advice. But from thirty I have! In the splendid authority of youth to youth I quote from those blurring pages, written in fierce swift pencil-passion: "You must be true to yourself. Strong enough to be true to yourself.

Brave enough, to be strong enough, to be true to yourself. Wise enough, to be brave enough, to be strong enough, to be true enough to shape yourself from what you actually are. What big words, O my Self: true, strong, brave and wise! But that's how it is, my Self. That's how it must be for you to walk steadily in your own ways, as gracefully as you feel, as upright as you feel, a ridiculous flower on top of your head, a sentimental daisy. For therein lies your individuality, your own authentic signature, the source of others' love for you."

·   ·   ·

Thank you again for your letters, my dear. I wish you a difficult year.

SYLVIA ASHTON-WARNER

September 29, 1966
New Zealand

· I ·

February, 1941 · Beginning of February. We're at our new school. It's at the top of the hill and you can see the river. We're so happy to be here.

The school building is not unlike the one on the Coast except that it has two rooms and is bigger. K has taken the smaller room for the senior children and has given me the big one for the small children. I just can't get over it that I am no longer working in an unlit small mean porch with a piece of blackboard on the wall among the coat pegs. I can't believe this tall ceiling, high rafters and a lot of air and echoes—for me to teach in. Tall windows, plenty of light, and blackboards on the walls legitimately with no coat pegs. And any number of desks, the old type with the seat and table part joined. Shabby but real. Strangely, I can move about.

Between my room and K's there's the small porch from which steep timber steps lead down outside. You get the feeling as you come up them that you necessarily rise to some upper level of being as well as to a higher floor and when you descend you feel the reverse.

K and I were fearfully excited this morning in our new school. We conversed in bated whispers as we met our new children, and their new faces. You find yourself looking inadvertently for the faces you knew as though they still lurked there somewhere, among these you don't know, as they lurk yet in the mind. I look for Hemi even though he had smashed the new lawnmower for no reason that I could see, beating at it with a stick till he cracked the wheels, and I still feel the presence of tall Hikirangi of the wild sweet voice who liked to hold my babies in school while she was doing her lessons and I myself was teaching, and I feel that any moment I'll see again the face of Hiho whose hair I cut one day and should not have. It seems that I want to see them among these strange ones, even the small face of Niki who pulled the skipping rope when Jonquil was skipping, that small face with its frizzy hair. But that face will endure for always.

Strange faces of children. Faces of these who have shared no experience with us except this first day. There's no common knowledge between us. These children know nothing of the dangerous tidal rivers on the Coast dividing us from civilization, of K's hazardous journeys along the beach to bring food and mail from the village, setting out at low tide, waiting there hours to return on the next low tide, arriving home with his horse and cart at some eerie hour of the night. These know nothing of the lamp I put in the window to guide him from the beach through the gap in the driftwood, nothing of the roar of the ocean in a storm; did not share with us the heavens of interdependence in that unsought isolation, or the bitter agonies of it.

Faces of children who have not yet, for good or ill, grown into our lives. Faces with no background or history to them for us, without even names until we learn them, paintings on paper, no more, with no deep dimension, or chalk drawings on a blackboard. No doubt our own faces are like that to them.

Unfamiliar faces. There was a time before we joined the Maori School Department when all Maori faces appeared the same, one brown face, but we know better now. There's as much variety in Maori features as there is in Europeans'. Each child is an entity, unique like us.

Clean faces too. Since, far from riding miles on horseback along the beach to school, down river valleys, over the ranges and fording swollen waters, these children merely stroll up from the village and are late at that.

But they are wonderful faces because from their new features I read over and over again that we are here, not there; no longer in That Other Place. I realize that here, in spite of the eighteen miles of river road, each corner named after the one who went over that particular cliff, we *could* get to our people—by riverboat, should the road be blocked. I read that our own civilization is at least represented here by a handful of white people, even though these faces do not yet reach into the mind to fuse with us.

"Funny, you know," I remarked to K this evening when we were bathing our babies, "these strange faces almost make me regret the ones we've left."

"I like these new children. I like the unknown."

"Daddy," from Jonquil, "I like them too. Because they like me. They all ran up to me, Daddy, and stared."

.   .   .

A week gone by. My baby, Dannie, is afraid of the new children. I've got to carry him to school with me as though he couldn't walk, whereas he walked very early for any baby and learned in a lighthouse where the woman took care of him when I was away. He can walk all right but he's frightened. The little chap clutches me . . . the darling.

.   .   .

I'm writing at my table in school while the children are writing. There's a girl here called Olga, about eight, who takes fits, falling to the floor and rolling her eyes. "Olga got a fit," the others call but only a few watch her. You take fits or you don't, and Olga does. Gosh she's a naughty girl, this Olga, and often hides my things but it's not that which annoys me: it's that smile on her face when she's asked about it, and when you find them, if you do.

She's a thin underfed girl reared on tea and biscuits from the Store, big dark eyes, black spiked hair and an ever-smiling mouth. Long dress and bare feet to match summing the overall wistfulness.

"Has anyone seen my scissors?" I asked.

"Please no."

"Don't say 'Please no.' My name is not Please. My name is Mrs. Henderson. Say 'No, Mrs. Henderson.' "

"Yes, M's Hen'son," from Jacob.

"You have? Where?"

"Please Olga hid it."

"Leave out the 'please,' Jacob. Just say, 'Olga hid it, Mrs. Henderson.' "

"Please I didn't," from Olga.

"Olga—say, 'I didn't, Mrs. Henderson.' "

"I didn't, M's Hen'son."

"Please she did," from Jacob.

"Can't you say, 'She did, Mrs. Henderson?' "

"She did, M's Hen'son."

"Did you see her?"

"Please yes."

"Where did she put it?"

"Please I don't know."

"But you must know, Jacob."

"Please I don't."

"Did anyone see where Olga hid my scissors?"

A delighted occasion to stop writing, the whole lot seeking industriously in any place where they knew the scissors would not be, and they'd still be looking had not Jonquil walked firmly to the wastepaper basket and extricated them.

Olga smiled.

Last night I dreamed I thrashed her for it, the smile, until she fell on the floor, yet she still smiled up at me. A nightmare I'd admit to no one.

But it's plain these children don't like me much; they all took Olga's side about the scissors.

· · ·

This school, though no more than within earshot of white civilization, is nevertheless more accessible to inspectors, which is a matter of disadvantage as well as advantage. One is obliged to return to orthodox methods. Back on that ocean beach at the foot of the ranges utterly beyond the frontiers of civilization I had begun to overturn the reading, the books supplied being quite irrelevant. In place of "the bed," "the can," and such, I'd made cards with words from their environment: beach, log, sand, cliff, ranges, fish, kit, lighthouse, shell, fight and horse, but here—back to the ridiculous books again. Such a retrograde step but after all it's the department that pays me and they who call the tune. I said to K at morning tea in my room this morning, "I'll have to make a whole new set of reading material now to support these dreadful books. That's the weakness of civilization—Don't you think so? You run into orthodoxy."

"We ourselves learned to read on worse books than that."

"That's a very good answer."

"It's the *way* you do a thing that matters, dear. I think. Not wholly the thing itself. That's what I've heard you say."

"That's a good answer too. Too good. Really I'm confused."

"Since you've got to use those books," he went on, rising, "there's no reason why you shouldn't put your individuality into your own manner of approach."

"But they're so boring!"

"Yes." He walked to the door.

"On the Coast they rather liked those words about the sea and the tide and that."

"Lucky," he called to one of his boys, "ring the bell, will you?"

"Please yes," said Lucky.

.　　.　　.

Still February. I can't believe it . . . that we're here and not there. Physically at least, and geographically. The pace of the soul is the walk of an ass and my soul is not all here yet. My soul is still reading poetry back on the Coast in order to survive. Oh forget it.

Lovely big house, bigger than that other. No it's not, it's smaller. Fewer rooms. It just *seems* bigger. Another old-timer that shares the top of the hill with the school dreaming out over the river below. Lovely place. During the depression, the Store man has told us, the Public Works Ministry put men on these grounds to give them jobs so that the grounds are laid out like a park. Strangely, all the blossoms are white, as though the foreman had been in love with a virgin. And circled with august trees: old-time skyscraper pines, stunning yellow-bloomed wattle and fruit trees planted before any depression, hoary and scaled with mosses and lichen. Enough fruit here to lay out the Japs should they ever arrive.

All you do to get to school is to pick up baby Dannie on one arm, holding dear Frannie by the hand and Jonquil following, and walk across the broken tennis court, all on the top of this hill like kings of the castle. And you look down on the river to assess its mood and around upon the surrounding wooded ranges to examine their mood, and sigh and kiss the baby. A secluded blue heaven to ourselves. And whom do you find at the school when you get there? No less than K.

"Good morning," as though we hadn't seen each other since yesterday after school.

"Oh . . . you're here?" turning from the blackboard.

I smile.

"I never cease to be surprised when I see you here."

"Dear, I love you."

Stand at his door with the three little ones.

"Look at that now."

He accompanies me and the babies into my infant room with its airiness and light. "I just can't get over it," I say, "that I've got all this room. You know? I can move about. They can move about. We can march and dance and all sorts. Can you believe it? And all that room on the wall blackboards. I say, I'll tell you what I want you to do. I want you to put a little rail along all those blackboards to hold their chalk."

"Please," from Lucky, "shall I ring the bell?"

.　　.　　.

This is evening with the children in bed and K back at school. I must get back to study soon. I've forgotten all I learned at training college about how to teach. All I can remember about teaching is how I myself was taught when young. That strict traditional way: spare the rod and spoil the child and that. And how we'd line up for reading and sums and get the strap if we got any wrong. The singsong tables in the morning and the strap for every spelling word wrong. All good at the time, I think, because we thought it was all right— and no one allowed to speak. But we didn't learn that at college. I've got to relearn what I was supposed to have learned. This very evening I mean to write a letter to the Country Library Service to get some books to study.

And not only for that reason. I don't mean to go down under marriage and babies as glamorous girls do, never to be heard of again. Down at heel, straggly hair and nothing important to say. I can't see why I need to. I can't see why marriage should wipe out my personality, why I should let it, I mean. Somehow . . . I don't know how what with home, school and family . . . I mean to recover and keep the things

I did when single; I mean some time to be what I had meant to be—in the first place a worthwhile person, not just for myself but for those who love me. I mean to so organize my loaded time that I'll retain some for myself to paint, do music, read and even learn to write. I'm not one of these people who were born for nothing.

I'm dreadfully tired. Now I'll go to bed and hope for a good night's sleep without Dannie waking, without a nightmare about the Coast, without anxiety about the war which might take K, without remembering in shame my anger at Olga—yes, anger, not mere irritation—without worrying about forgetting how to teach, if I ever knew, without bleakly counting my bead-dreams that I dreamed when I was single about how I would live my life: a glamorous mysterious vivid life in the capitals of the world with those of my own kind—artists, musicians and writers. And lovers demanding a look from me, and friends thinking me wonderful. Paris, Rome, New York . . . roaming, roaming, fascinated. Getting on and off ships and trains and planes, the last word in fashion. Without remembering those dreams and seeing them against what I am now: a forgotten girl on the top of a hill drearily teaching Maoris. A forgotten girl.

. . .

"Jacob, have you finished your work?"

"Please no."

"Tiny has. Look, all that." I held up Tiny's exercise.

"Please she copied it off . . . off—" glancing about him experimentally—"off Whitu."

"Please I didn't," from Tiny. "Please I copied it out of myself."

"Jacob, bring me your exercise book. Let me see it."

"Please I . . . please it's not here."

"Where is it?"

"Please at home."

"I told you not to take your book home. You'll have to go home and get it. Up you get . . . off! Go home and get your book."

"Please I can't."

"You've got legs!"

"Please yes. But the canoe it's not there."

"What's the canoe got to do with it?"

"My grandfather took it."

"Where?"

"Please he took our canoe downriver to the other pa because there's a tangi there because a man got drowned last night. He was eeling."

"What have *eels* got to do with your exercise book?"

Tiny beside me, who is truly tiny like a little black beetle, said, "Please Jacob he live on the other side of the river. He comes to school in the canoe."

"Am I to believe that a boy of Jacob's size goes to and fro across that wide deep river in a canoe every day?"

"Please, my big sisters bring me. They in Mr. Hen'son's room."

I paused. I'd lost the thread. With elbow on table I covered my eyes with a hand while I tried to find it again but all I could see in my mind were canoes, drowned men, eels and a grandfather. "What was I talking about, Tiny?"

She brushed the black hair from her eyes. "Please about Jacob he hasn't did his writing."

Mercifully the bell rang for morning play.

"Jacob," I said, "here's some paper. You stay in and do your writing."

"Please I can't write outside of inside myself like Tiny."

Baffled. "Look. Don't any of you children know my name yet?"

"Please yes."

"Please stop calling me Please!"

They looked puzzled.

"What is my name?" I said.

"Please M's Hen'son."

"Just answer 'Mrs. Henderson.' "

Chorus, "Jus' answer M's Hen'son."

"*Mrs. Henderson.*"

"M's Hen'son."

"*Now* do you know it?"

"Please yes."

If you can call that teaching.

"Really," to K over morning tea, "my teaching. I haven't *started* to teach. There's no communication. We're supposed to be using the same language but we just don't understand each other. I dunno . . .'"

"I'll give you an outline of a lesson. Now for a writing lesson you . . ."

"But you see they're not thinking about what they're writing about or about what I'm teaching. I'm teaching about 'bed' and 'can' but they were thinking about canoes and grandfathers and drowned men and eels. It seems to me . . . I seem to be *rude* to *intrude.*"

"That's just it. Well, dear, that's what we're paid to do, just that: intrude."

. . .

Intrude. For once I won't intrude. It's really time for reading about the bed, the can, and I can jump, I can skip and I can run. But I can't bring myself to do it. I'll follow them into their own minds and fraternize there; their minds are full of grandfathers, canoes and eels and the river and so, indeed, is mine. I call them to my feet for a story, swiftly improvising:

. . .

Once upon a time there lived a boy called Jacob on the other side of the river. He liked to write in his writing book and show it to the teacher but one morning he forgot to take it. He couldn't go back and get his book because Grandpa had the canoe. What shall I do about it? he thought, walking up to school.

Just at that moment who should pass but Diggetty-Dig the Dog. "Hey, Diggetty-Dig," Jacob said, "I've left my book behind. Will you swim back and get it?"

"I'll risk it, if you like," replied the dog, "but it's not a good idea. Grampitty is shooting ducks today and might shoot me instead. He doesn't see too well."

Back he swam across the river and ran to Jacob's place where he found the book upon the bed and settled down to read it. He read one page and then another and turned over to the next. Not bad for Jacob, Diggetty thought, but I can write much better. He wrote a page in it himself for Jacob to show the teacher and signed his name in capital letters, DIGGETTY-DIG THE DOG.

Then taking the book in his mouth he swam back across the water, but seeing Grampitty in the canoe he dropped the book on a floating log and made off fast for cover.

Dippetty-Dip the Duck appeared. There's Jacob's book, she thought. I'll take it to him. But first of all she wrote a page and signed her name to it, then, taking the book in her bill, flew off across the water until she heard Grampitty's voice, at which she dropped the book upon a rock and flapped toward the trees.

Slippetty-Slip the Eel slid near and he too wrote a page, signed his name, took the book and set off after Jacob, but at the sound of Grampitty's gun he flicked the book upon the bank and slid off under water.

All morning the book lay on the bank for anyone to write in, even Flippetty-Flip the Flea, but as he didn't write too well he drew some pictures in it, not forgetting to sign his pretty name. FLIPPETTY-FLIP THE FLEA, until in the afternoon who should come along but Grampitty-Gramp himself, it being time to return the canoe and tie it up for Jacob.

"By crikey me," said Grampitty-Gramp, "that book belongs to Jacob." But he didn't write a page himself as he couldn't see well.

Up at the school the teacher said, "Now children, do your writing." So the children all began to write but Jacob had no book. I left my book at home, he thought, and I couldn't go back to get it.

Just at that moment what should he hear but a soft knock on the door, and who should he see but Grampitty-Gramp with Booketty in his hand.

"You brought my book, Grampitty-Gramp! Now I can do my writing."

But when Jacob opened his book to write, all he could do was read. He read the pages the others had written and all their capital letters. DIGGETTY-DIG THE DOG, he read, and DIP-PETTY-DIP THE DUCK, and SLIPPETTY-SLIP THE EEL, he read, and FLIPPETTY-FLIP THE FLEA. He found out all about his book since he left her behind that morning.

"Poor little Booketty-Book," he said. "I left you behind this morning."

He did no writing in his book, for the others had done it for him. Diggetty-Dig the Dog had done it and Dippetty-Dip the Duck; and Slippetty-Slip the Eel had done it and Flippetty-Flip the Flea. He smiled as he took up their clever work and showed it to the teacher.

·   ·   ·

Glancing down upon Jacob's tears I know I have not intruded, that I have fraternized with him. I see in his large brown upturned eyes the potential of a good boy. A boy you could get at. A boy with response. A boy you could lead into being what a boy should be, through affection; wanting to do what you wanted. A boy in whom all things are possible.

But life goes on, teaching goes on and reading goes on and a teacher herself must obey the curriculum. My grading will be very bad if they can't read their books and I'll be called a poor teacher. As the children get out their reading books and I go to the blackboard here is the bed and the can again and all about I can jump. As my chalk rebels a moment, a flash of insight comes: I'm turning Jacob into a naughty boy.

Sunday, February 23 · A Maori party last night over the way, singing, stamping and clapping all night and, with an interval for sleep in the morning, all today too. I can hear them at it now. The Maori way of blowing off steam, and when they have spent themselves they'll turn back into just quiet harmless folk again. A pity some Europeans don't take a little of the same treatment instead of hoarding emotion, let all the evil and venom and passion and weeping escape; then they would be harmless too.

This morning was so like a dream. Late breakfast, then we lay in the sun of the valley among the fruit and wattle trees with the soft forest at hand, the dream-blue sky filling our eyes, and the singing of the Maoris. I lay on my back eating a pear, my eyes drowning in the brilliant yellow of the wattle, saying over and over. "It's like a dream, it's like a dream."

In the afternoon I ran away from the family, lay barebacked, barefoot with my book among the trees and read and slept. I felt like a child again after the nightmare of the Coast. The harmony of this place, I thought, the harmony between us and everyone we have met so far, the bush, the sky, the river and the Maoris. How terrible That Other Place I realize only now. With my face in the kind grass I felt happy enough to return to the children again.

February 24 · Boy Two says "klums" for plums, Boy Three says for Whanganui River, "Mommelly River." The darlings.

Busy I've been at odd intervals making school material,

painting, drawing, sawing timber and even mixing concrete—mainly stuff for my number scheme. Somehow I must teach these children number or they'll be teaching me. Who knows? I might learn to count.

Saturday, March 1 · K did the washing and I baked all morning, scones and quite good pikelets. In the afternoon I dressed up, ostensibly to visit the sick Mrs. Hira, but actually hoping to see white people in the village. The lovely white linen suit, backless, bare legs, white sandals with the cord winding round the ankle—too smart for life on the river? . . . but no one at the House answered my knock, neither did Mrs. W. at the Store so, in fact, I did visit the sick, two hours of it with decomposing Mrs. Hira in her bed in the whare across the graveyard, or three. She was very ill today and I ran out of cigarettes, which I relied on for disinfectant.

But coming back, too disappointed, I avoided the crowd waiting at the Store for their mail and lurked down the river road round the corner until they had gone. Reading "Il Penseroso" and Dryden's "The Power of Music." An unhappy afternoon.

When they had all gone I still couldn't raise the W.'s at the Store, was too curled up with hurt to try the House again, so I walked slowly back up through the village reading Dryden till I reached home on the hill where Jonquil ran out of the nursery to me and where K kissed me closely. Through the lovely tea he gave me we were carried forward on the wave of emotion between us. "You must always," he said, "open your arms to me when I come for you because it's like opening your heart to me . . ." on the wave of emotion to its ultimate conclusion. "You would," I said afterward, "only say those things to me, wouldn't you?"

"Because they are for you."

Sunday, March 2 · The next day, Sunday, K stays home with the three little ones while I get on with my renewal of acquaintance with white people. He goes on making the fowlhouse while I go riding with Mrs. Sands, who brought me a horse. This extraordinary reintroduction to white people— I've forgotten the techniques. We rode to the top of the up-river road to the deserted cottage where we watered our horses. She was far from being my own kind, being full of her operations and her scrapes with death but she had a clean tongue and was free of gossip. We galloped back to lunch at her place and I got home about five. How wonderful to see the children again—what a change a few hours away can make!

Mrs. Hira sent me a New Testament in Maori which I keep high up on top of the radio until I've investigated the question of TB contagion.

March 4 · I have so much to do between school and home that I have to give every minute its value. I must keep my reading and learning of poetry going and mental exercises, Huxley, Russell and such, from the public library and the new book clubs; one book at least has been suitable: *This Hill Is Mine*. Also there is the Maori language to continue learning, school work, scheme, workbook and chart preparation. I practice Maori sentences that Mrs. Hira has taught me, over and over again, whenever I'm alone, doing dishes or sweeping. Whenever I rest I pick up my novel and last thing at night I read one poem.

I do my school work in the afternoon and after tea. I paint charts in the conglomerate sun porch, but still there's a book to be written; every night, dead or dying, after school work and letters, I get in those few lines.

K taught the children to replace a slight whine with a particularly dulcet tone which they are keen enough to use when they want something really. When he was bathing the children and washing Three's neck, "Daddy, don't choke my neck," in the sweetest tone.

"But I have to wash your neck, Frannie."

"Don't choke my neck, Daddy," in the pleasantest key. "You're choking my neck, Daddy." By then it was clean.

"I asked the big boys at school," K told me, "what they usually did on Friday afternoon before we came. They said, 'Chop wood, sir.' " K looked at me and I roared with laughter. "I thought," he went on, "is it possible that I don't have to coach these big boys to chop wood?"

Boy Two says "punning" for "pudding."

March 5 · The children at school are bursting at the skin with all this violent spirit, held in check for teaching purposes only by the finest strategy, and then not always, but let loose legitimately in the widespread games that K is able to teach them. Even so it explodes at times of their choosing rather than ours, like an enemy mine in the battlefields in Crete, where our New Zealand Division is. True, we also call for the blood-hot dances, the hakas, to clear a lot of it out, but oh, the vim of the Maoris against the silence, the poker silence, of the poor little white children. Both vim and violence start with *v* but silence starts with *s*, a noncommittal letter.

The lady at the House told K last night that when the nurse returns she will bring her over to meet me . . . well, well! *Me!* With a white lady visitor and educated too. Many a long day, a bleak year, since a thing like that has happened. Not since we left civilization over three years ago.

March 6 · My two little boys, Three and Two, backfired into school today, both crying and bleeding from a fall down the steps, and although I was teaching something important, number, I dismissed my classes and took the babies home and dressed their little wounds. I put them in the big chair and gave them tea. Never would this have happened had I not been teaching. To me, never will teaching be other than a necessary source of income, a profession drifted into on account of the hours, the holidays and the fact that others did it. *Never!*

Sunday, March 9 · Among the things about K that astound me is the way he takes his teaching seriously as though it were something other than a source of income. Up close it looks as if his work is also his *hobby*. At college we called it sheer betrayal. I don't know how he can be so *open* about it! At school he's a headmaster and not my husband. For all that, however, I did drift into a drawing lesson with his seniors while he took my little ones for wonderful games on the lawn outside, so that when he came in afterwards and saw for himself that his big ones were busy and happy he was as amazed as they were and as I was too, at what was happening beneath their fingers. Big daisies, yellow-centered, petals red-tipped, serrated with the sun and the shadow on them. In a low voice looking about, "This is what I love to see . . . activity. Do you like it?"

"Yes I do," surprised.

Approval from my headmaster. "Do you think it is good?" begged the wife.

"Of course I do," finish.

Oh, why can't he kiss me? Will I ever accustom myself to no applause . . . well, not enough, I mean? And will I ever get used to my lover-husband turning into a cold headmaster?

. . .

The nurse came to the school today under her own power, with the supervising nurse. I saw them through the door and went out, my mind all but blacked out with curiosity. Terribly nervous, I put on my old show of plenty to say and brightness, damn it. Took them over to the house, forgot the key, fumbled with the stove and stammered over words until K came and took over . . . all because of the *poise* of the nurse. How I envied her! Poise is the first casualty in isolation. Desperately I envied her. Here was no fear of anyone. An untroubled gaze before which my own eyes dropped nervously again and again. Gave way. The moment K took over the conversation—his poise has survived—I relapsed most thankfully into my nonfavorite role of listener so that by the time he went and left me to it I'd collected myself sufficiently to *direct* the conversation while they indulged in the actual *talking*.

March 11 · The next morning, walking over to school, I tried to be strong enough not to give in to the allurement of the new piano—there's got to be a piano wherever I teach—beneath the old-time window, not to sink my hungry fingers into the luxurious keys and try to remember the "Viennese Dance," but at the sight of it I collapsed and lifted the lid and here was this Friedmann in a Maori schoolroom . . . incongruity indeed. In the woodwork was reflected my scarlet cardigan, on the top of my head the disorganizing sun and in my ears the remembered rhythm with its revolutionary magic until I found myself thinking, Even if this is the sin of dreaming in the morning of reality, the sin of lifting myself from the ground to the forbidden heaven when I should be preparing my work . . . this sin is worth it. Oh for the day when I can drop this teaching and spend the hours at music. . . . This wretched profession that cuts the spirit to splinters.

But I managed to close the piano and when I went to the blackboard and felt the shock of the cool of reality I knew I mustn't do that again, and not only on account of school; I was diluting my appetite for the legitimate time—if I could find the legitimate time.

· · ·

Violence. The word beginning with a capital *V* widespread across the world. The violence I believe to be in all of us subdued in the undermind, waiting, but which blasts out on occasion depending on how near the surface it is, or on the rigidity of the surface. Nearing ten o'clock there were still only eight children at school until the balance strolled in, apparently doing us a favor. The nonchalance of this race! K went outside to reprove them but ended up merely talking to them, while I, waiting inside, compared the unrelieved pace at home from five o'clock on, just to be in time for them, with the hours they dawdled away in the village and still managed to be late. K let the whole lot off, but when mine came in from roll call I didn't let them off. I stood them out on the floor and did I let them have it! I lashed with my tongue all round as I lash in my nightmares with a stick all round until there's no stick left. "No thin edge of the wedge for me! You can't put on your act with me! I know you lazy Maoris!" The insults spun like shrapnel.

After the brawl I felt a bit better, at least I suppose I did, but the mood of rage persisted all through the following lesson—the teaching of a tender song about flower buds in the spring: "In their tiny cradles, just above the ground . . ." through the bright tears of many of them. "Listen . . . like this: 'In their tiny cradles,'" I sang above my rage, "'just above the ground . . .'" while hollowly strummed the ukulele. "Come here, Pearly, you're not listening." Through the tears the voices sang on, " 'Softer, sweeter beds than these never could be found.' " K himself paid and let them off but with me *they* will pay. Not I any more. I saw Eva furtively studying me, with curiosity examining my face . . . perhaps I no longer looked lovely.

"Mine got it this morning," I said to K as we sat down to lunch at home.

"Oh, I prefer to give them another chance."

· · ·

It is still March when Jonquil says to me, "Mummie, the children over there don't like me. They liked me for a while when I first came but now they don't like me, Mummie."

"If you are kind and gentle they will like you." What about my own performance last week? How can they like *me?*

Yet life has a glow and a glamour, a sort of secret pulse. Here we are, all together starting our new life, sound in wind, limb and mind . . . almost enclosed at the top of a hill. A wonderful thing to be all together to those who have known separation, to be starting life all over again with a valley of shadows behind you. We've got as far as March already, three months since we came, but the radiance and the wonder inform the drama in the front line of action still.

The faces at school are changing. No longer are they chalk drawings on a blackboard but faces of identities with three dimensions and beginning to mean something to us—their minds fusing ever so briefly with what is in ours. Already they are faces which have shared with us a short important experience; they are part of our coming to the river, of our return from the wilderness.

In, out, above and below the pace of living and teaching we know that we are young; that the life ahead is ours, that we can make a stunning thing of it as long as we're together.

True, there's a terrible war on with our division in the thick and the heat of it, to which K could well be called and, true, I instinctively hate this teaching business with its imposition of oneself upon others, but there remains in our blood this steady excitement, this hot pulsing of energy. Together and here, we're sure we can accomplish anything at all, can *make* life into what we want. "To him who works," I read in Tennyson, "this grand year is ever at the doors."

But I wish I could see more order in progress. I'd like to be able to say in March, Look, I've got this far. I've taken one step to somewhere. To say, My teaching has obviously improved. *I* have obviously improved. Now I'll engage in the next step. But I can't, really. At school the number and reading are worse and the children's behavior too, and at home the pace is tenser, making my own behavior at school no better than the children's. I don't seem to know how to teach at all after two whole years at training college and several years in the classroom. After a weekend of impassioned preparation of material I find myself on the Monday morning lining up a row of small children each with a book in his hands, to come and read a line to me, or perhaps a page. Then it's over, the reading. Where do you go from here?

You'd think there'd be a marvelous reading lesson running into half an hour after all that work. What do I do next? They're idle, naughty and frightened of me, yet I deserve better than that. "Go back to your seat, Olga, you naughty girl, and leave Tiny's things alone."

"Please Tiny she got my reading book. Tha's mine."

"Please no," from Tiny, brushing back her hair. "It's mine."

"Stop that fooling, Jacob, and read your book."

"Please Olga she hid my book."

Olga smiles. "Please no, I didn."

"Pearly, pick up your book from the floor. Don't stand on it! You don't stand on books, you read them."

"Please tha's not my book," from Pearly. "It's Jacob's."

Pearly is Rosie Tahore's small sister, with the same fair curly hair.

"Jacob, is that the way to treat your book? Pick it up and read it. Look after your reading book, you naughty boy."

He picks it up and examines it.

"Is that your book?" I ask.

"Shess."

"Say 'Yes, Mrs. Henderson.' "

"Yes, M's Hen'son."

"Hen-der-son."

"Hen-*der*-son. Please Pearly she threw my book on the floor."

"Pleaseno," from Pearly.

"Shess," from Jacob.

"Sno," from Pearly.

"Shess."

"Sno."

The disrespect of this race for books, for the written word, and indeed for me. In the place where interest in books should be is an echoing hollow. A wrangle rather than reading.

The only time they show any sign of interest is when I let them draw, when it seems that furtively they let escape the pictures rampant in the mind—these pictures in the mind that offend so, that disorganize real teaching. If only their black heads had nothing whatever in them, then all I would have to do is fill them up. Its what's in their minds that makes them revolt. Empty children couldn't be naughty.

Or when I tell them a story. They attend to me then and sit wonderfully still. It seems then that their minds and my mind become one thing, two friends arm in arm. Sometimes I tell them a story about what I know they're thinking, but today I told them a story about what I was thinking, being short on shared experience. They don't know the Coast by the lonely ocean, not as those other children did, or of how we got there. I suspect they think that I don't know what real living is like, seeing me as no more than a smart dressed-up walkie-talkie doll called a teacher, with legs, arms, body and a face and shiny curly hair. Whereas if they knew me as a person, if I knew them as persons, they might like me and I like them, so that these long fierce hours in school might cease to be front-line action and become gentle inspiring interchange . . . *O doloroso.*

On Wednesday when K took my little ones for games out-side and I took his big girls for sewing and they hadn't brought their sugarbags to start on, all of us worn out with just the thought of sewing anything at all, a wary conversa-tion escaped and I told them a little of the Coast—the isola-tion, the ocean the tidal rivers and the lamp I would put in the window at night to guide K along the beach and up through the driftwood—so that big Rosie Tahore stopped being a tricky recalcitrant schoolgirl and became for the moment a brown-eyed friend who felt what I was telling them with all of herself and plainly wanted to. And sleek Caroline with the long black plaits and a long eye for the boys forgot about the boys pro tem. And Mere and Harriet, Jacob's sisters who bring him to school in the canoe, two slim graceful pretty things with very good English . . . well there was no sew-ing. In place of sly girls there were receptive women.

"Please," from Rosie, "the beach an the tidal rivers. An no road. Please how did you get there?"

"I'll tell you some day, Rosie."

Caroline, "Please tell us now."

"Shess, shess," from Mere and Harriet.

"Shess," from Caroline.

"Shess," from Rosie.

Rosie Tahore the tall, with the large loose dark-pink lips, the light-brown eyes, the light-brown skin and the un-Maori fair hair—an inheritance from some past fusion of the black hair and the golden—I'll tell her some day.

Harriet is terribly pretty. "Please tell us now," she says.

"I may tell you some day," I reply with propriety, "when you have brought your sugarbags."

Hellen is bigger than Rosie. In her past was no union of the black hair and the golden. Hellen is Maori undiluted. She's buxom and big and charming. Her hair is short, straight and inky, her eyes like the darkest night set in paper-pure whites, her teeth chalk-white. Hellen I'll tell anything one day, should the disciplines of school not divide us: I, the teacher . . . you, the pupil. I am greater than thou. She speaks well.

"Please I hate sewing," from Hellen.

"You can't call a sugarbag sewing. All you do is—"

"My mother hasn't got a sugarbag."

"What do you buy your sugar in then?"

"Please in a sugarbag. But my mother keeps them for when she goes eeling. To carry the eels in."

Back to the eels in the river again. Nothing to do with sewing.

My voice lifts, and my hands. "I hear so much about these eels," I say, "that you ought to bring some to school. I'd put them on the roll and sit them at a desk." A laugh from the girls. "You know what I'd teach them?" my hands throwing about. "I'd teach the eels to sew!"

If you can call that teaching . . .

Yes, it is late. I'm writing at the kitchen table and the babies are all asleep, and I'm very tired. But life still has this glow and glamour, this secret hot beat of the pulse. To us, together, all is possible. We don't always remember this during the day engaged in front-line action, but we do again in moments of solitude. The certainty that our life is ours, that the future is ours, that the world belongs to us who are young, that Fate is an obedient servant; and that happiness, if not picked up on the roadside, can be *made* with our own hands.

> Ah, make the most of what we yet may spend,
> Before we too into the Dust descend; . . .

Dannie is as unsettled as ever. All Frannie did was sing to-ward the house, "Teatime, teatime," finally working into "Tea-tom, tea-tom."

"Don't say 'tea-tom'" from Dannie.

"Tea-tom, tea-tom . . ."

Dannie, louder, "Don't say 'tea-tom!'"

"Tea-tom, tea-tom, tea—"

A roar of rage, "Don't!"

Out come Dannie's fists and a big fight follows.

But lately he's had a few days of light, making quite a different world for us; supersweet he can be, with overwhelming fascination. When he's in such a mood it's easy to be gentle. This morning he held this happy mood from waking up till school time as he watched me doing the ironing, and I held it too, for as K left for school he turned and said, "There's no one can do a shirt as you can, dear."

My mood held right into school when the nurse came again. Through the window I could not mistake the carriage of her head even had the children not rushed in and said, "Nurse is out there, Mrs. Henderson!" For she was so friendly and I more at ease, looking her more squarely in the eyes this time . . . beautiful eyes they are. But how can I explain to each white person here the reason of my shyness—that I've come from a place of no white faces?

But whatever Dannie's rages of the day, he says in the nurs-ery at bedtime, "Make me storwee, Mummie."

For it's usually I with the children in the evening as there's always something to call K out: three Home Guard parades a week or the mail to be got from the Store—a pacifying business now. No longer the journey by horse and cart along the tidal beaches, or the lamp to light in the window. He brought home Mr. Snowdon's rifle the other day—a rifle in K's hands and in our home, incongruous sight. He let the children hold it, at which I started in horror—the big malicious thing in their soft hands. How connect the thought of killing with K

and the children? As for me, never having touched one in my
life, I was amazed at the weight of it.

March 18 · Francis, always wanting to be cuddled, follows
me to and fro with his arms round my knees when I'm at work
in the kitchen, slowing me tenderly down. He's the one who
talks to himself, his imagination seeming to take charge completely. He has this way of looking upward and away from his
surroundings so that one learns to expect from this far-off
look some fairy-tale. When K has lost something and asks
Francis where it is, his fabrications are incredible.

I'm forever tying up their cuts and pricks and all their sudden bruises and need a supply of bandages. I don't know
which is the more arduous—keeping track of their shoes and
socks or keeping level with the first aid. Either is close on a
full-time job. Their shoes are wet, or lost, or they want them
done up and they change shoes with each other continually.
To such a point does it slow you down that you learn that
faithful adherence to any program in a house of children is
quite beyond attainment.

As for the questions alone—well, they've got to be answered. "Mummie," from Jon, "where is the end of the
world?"

"There's no end to the world, my darling. It just goes
round and round like a ball."

"Oh I see. Got its ends tied up."

On occasion, however, I do slip down for an hour to the
nurse's cottage where Jean Humphrey exercises her profession
of "looking after people" although I shy away from any reference to myself with an inclination that is becoming natural,
fortunately. At last I am beginning to learn—after the Coast—
that others are not compulsively interested in me, whatever
they say or leave unsaid.

July · In late July the house is full of the fragrance of the first spring flowers . . . I can't hate anyone amidst such glory. The spring is here, my beloved is here and our children are strong and growing. And always this pressing forward, this reaching, striving . . . something driving toward its object, so slowly, yet nevertheless going forward with each formed thought and written word. "That creative force," says Havelock Ellis, "which gives us no rest until we have finally given it representation."

And when from force of domesticity or some emotional upset there is a lull in its drive I need but go to the piano and follow Friedmann through his "Viennese Dance" to recover it again; or when K is stirring the porridge, to move to the stove myself for something, when occurs one of those inexplicable moments with us in each other's arms.

"Anyway," he says against my face, "we love each other."

"I'm only a poor artist. You can't expect anything of me."

"Other couples teaching together were quarreling with each other only three months after they started. We've been three years and we've only begun."

"I claim I compare pretty well with the rest of the wives— even though I'm not a good teacher."

"You do! You do! It doesn't matter how far we fall, we always come to the bedrock of loving each other. It's something we can't fall past." Passionate kisses over the porridge. And later in the school where I was settling in for my day's study and he was making the fire burn for me, he kissed me again and said he loved me, so that over the years behind I saw clearly the face of the man that had bounded my horizon at that time and in his eyes that same look I had craved with all my willful youth . . . that concentrated intensity that men call ageless. Laying his hand on my head he said, "This is not hair, my darling; this is the work of an experienced silk-worm."

August · Spring in August finds the little ones bringing me jonquils growing wild in the nooks of the valley, and Frannie brought a budding carnation. Even Jean sent, but did not bring, some Iceland poppies from town. Had she brought them herself I would have forgotten everything of the disharmony between us, but they still looked lovely for all that in the green translucent vase, against the orange and green of the kitchen. Detached, their beauty from the drama of life, dissolving current strains. They pull the wild eye outward from the tumults within to softly revive the vision. Abuse for no one when I went to school.

True, Hellen was late again but her arms were loaded with jonquils, jostling with wild daffodils. "Why are you late again," I asked, "after the very same thing yesterday?"

The dark Maori tumbled the vivid flowers into my opening arms. "They were growing in the paddocks, Mrs. Hen'son. All over the paddocks."

"Go and tell Mr. Henderson why you're late, and thank you for the flowers."

. . .

But although spring is benevolent, rages remain. With dreams crashing in on reality and reality crashing in on dreaming during the hours before school, I'm in an exclusive rage when I get there to find Rosina and Rosie Tahore late, Tiny's nails dirty and somebody's teeth unbrushed. How I went for them! I flung my tongue round like a cat-o'-nine-tails so that my pleasant peaceful infant room became little less than a German concentration camp as I took out on the children what life should have got. Moreover, Frannie was sick today, lying on a bed of cushions by the big school fire where he slept and wept alternately until I dismissed my classes early, carried my lamb home and nursed him like a mother. If only I were not teaching . . .

Yet they've receded lately, the nightmares, when hidden in sleep I beat the children, not with my tongue at all but with a stick till it breaks into the smallest pieces, too small to use. No, not from the tenderness of spring in the flowered, forested valley and not only from my concentrated study but from something strangely new: tentatively, reluctantly, I'm becoming interested in no less than my infant room. From the reading I do in the early hours before the household wakes, how could I not become interested? Freud, Adler, Lipmann, Scheiner, Jung and Bertrand Russell explaining life and children, and all the poetry at night. I am my own University, I my own Professor.

Is it possible that teaching small children could be more than a source of income, more than a way of paying your bills? Today, remembering the people I read, no longer able to bear my shame at growling at little children, I turned my ever-seeking mind toward evolving some system of marks: ticks for good behavior, crosses for bad, with the result that all day my tongue has not got away. Yet never have I had a better-mannered class, or better work either. Spring after the atrocious winter it could be, more careful planning, but mainly the study I do. At last I'm beginning to extricate myself from the only conception of teaching I remembered since I resumed on the Coast—the manner in which I was taught myself—and am recollecting what I learned in college. It was latent there all the time.

Also I have been taking more pains to look nice for K: freshly ironed smock, lipstick, comb and powder in the cupboard and a release of smiles. Sitting over the schoolroom fire at morning tea he said, "You're looking very nice this morning."

"That won't do."

"Why?"

"I might be betrayed," at which we laughed.

•   •   •

Really . . . poor little Pearly trying to get a tick today.
The whole of her pale-brown soul concentrated on it. When
she was writing her spelling her tongue accompanied her cir-
cuitous thinking, her face lowered out of sight as though she
were actually writing with this tongue, and her feet stuck out
in front of her halfway across the room. Big wide cracked
feet, weather- and leather-resistant.

Pearly is like her big sister Rosie who is in the senior room.
The same fair curls on the pale-brown skin, the large loose
dark-pink lips, but she hasn't the grace of Rosie Tahore who
ambles dreamfully, moving with slowness from A to B as
though she had weeks to get there, and thinking of dark-pink
matters. She hasn't the grace of Rosie. Pearly has feet that are
far too big in my terms of reference, always bare, of course,
unlike the princess feet of Mere and her sister Harriet who
live across the river, or their small brother Jacob. She doesn't
seem to know what to do with them, they seem to be something extra, getting in her own way, as well as everyone else's.
One foot trips over the other foot, and both trip over everything.

"Pearly, be a good girl and tuck your feet underneath the
desk. So we won't trip over."

She looks up, pained. Her gold-brown eyes usually have
this look of recurring bewilderment, as though each minute of
life were a minute of problem about what to do with her feet.

"Please a tick?" she says with advancement in mind.

"What, for just pulling your feet in, a tick?"

"Shess."

I almost reply "Sno." They're still stretched out and at this
moment white Bernard falls upon them. "Well, I don't know

about a tick for just pulling your feet in." She's more likely to get a cross for having them out.

They remain sprawled. Two enormous feet for a little girl —fascinating. "Look," I suggest, "the other children all have their feet tucked in."

Several pairs of feet are swiftly tucked under while Bernard gets up and examines a knee.

"Please," says Tiny of the fairy feet, "Pearly she haven got a shoes. Please her feets too wide. Please her mother she take Pearly to town for a shoes an please the man he carn make a shoes to get on Pearly her feets."

Pearly looks over her desk at her feet protruding well beyond her and examines them with pain. "They's wide," she admits with sorrow.

"I don't mean she has to wear shoes. I didn't say they were big. All I want is room to walk without tripping over."

"Please they's big," from Pearly.

"Please," from Tiny, "the man he said her feets they like two wheelbarrows."

Pearly stares at them, concerned, and wistful about it all, then looks at Tiny's feet. "Please Tiny her feets theys far too small. Theys little like a fantail."

The conversation has veered a long way from the subject in hand, to wit, their spelling on the blackboard; bed, can, train and horse have little to do with fantails and feet, so I struggle back to the point of departure. "Pearly, you tuck in your feet so Bernard won't fall over."

She recovers her point of departure. "Please I get a tick?"

"Oh . . . yes . . . *one.*"

Back goes one foot under the desk, "Now the other, Pearly."

"Please two tick?"

"Good heavens, no!"

I'm confused. For some reason, as I glance about, many other feet suddenly stick out: the new system is working all too well. "What are all your feet sticking out for? How can I pass to see your work? I'll break my neck."

"Pleaseatick?"

I've had enough of these feet sequences and am about to raise my voice in authority—Put all those feet out of sight or else—but some echo from training college, some line from Freud I've been plowing through, or Jung or Adler or Russell . . . what was it? There's something here I should know. I sense a warning I don't understand, but you can't go around all day giving ticks for no more than pulling your feet in, the thing would get out of hand. I mean . . . the next thing you'd be giving ticks for coming to school at all, you'd be giving ticks for breathing and a cross for not breathing, besides I am the teacher and they're supposed to do what I say. Deep breath but nothing to say.

Olga sympathizes. "Too many feets ay."

"Far too many." And far too far from the spelling lesson.

"Please," from Jacob, who speaks good English (I've found out that his grandfather is actually a minister), "my grandfather he's got big feet."

"Leave old Grampitty out of it, Jacob."

"Pearly her father he got a big feets," from industrious little Tiny. She brushes back the tail of hair permanently across her eyes, and sniffs philosophically. "Please he carry the kumara* on his feets. Pearly her mother she said Pearly her father he can build a big house on one of his feets."

"Please M's Hen'son," from Olga again, "my father he said that Pearly her father his feet theys big enough for a dance hall."

Andrew joins in with pride. "Please my mother she was at the dance hall on Saturday and my mother she was drunk. Please she thrash my uncle. An my uncle he cried an he said to my mother, 'You don' love me now. I drown myself in the river.' An Mando she run down to the river and she say to my

* Kumara: sweet potato

uncle, 'You drown yourself, Uncle.' And my uncle he said, 'Yes the eels they can have me. Or the taniwha.' " *

"Please Andrew's mother," says white Bernard, "isn't married to Andrew's father. His father likes the white girl at the River House."

"Shess . . . shess!"

"What's the name," I ask, "of the white girl at the River House?"

"Undine."

"Shess."

"Shess."

"What's your father's name, Andrew?"

"Wingo."

Wingo and Undine . . . poetry itself. I'm electrocuted. The bell goes for playtime, fortunately.

.   .   .

I feel so keenly the distance between us, not only between what I am trying to teach and what they are thinking about but between my mind and the children's. It's not a friendly feeling. In the afternoon at story time I make an effort to reach out and mingle with them. In any case I have no choice, since all I can think of is feet and Pearly and the water monster in the river. "Once upon a time," I begin in doubt, "There was . . . let me see . . ."

An enthralled silence falls.

"Once upon a time there was a girl called Pearly who had rather nice feet. Some said that they were big but—" Stalled again. I don't know what comes next.

Silence . . . magic.

"One morning when Pearly was walking by the river she saw something in the water. What was it? Guess what she saw in the water, can you?"

"Sno."

* Taniwha: a lengendary monster in the river

"Have a guess," I said.

"Eels?"

"No."

"Ducks?"

"No."

"Canoe?"

"No. She saw the taniwha, the water monster in the river.

"Oo-oo-ooh!"

"Now look, I'll start this story again."

. . .

Once upon a time there was a girl called Pearly who had rather nice feet. Some people said they were far too big but I didn't think so at all. It was only because she stuck them out and the children tripped upon them. The boys tripped over, the girls tripped over and even the teacher too.

If only they were not so big, she thought, they would stop sticking out. They get bruised with all this kicking. I think I'll stop coming to school.

One morning when Pearly was walking by the river instead of going to school she noticed a ripple in the water and, taking a closer look, she recognized the taniwha, the water monster in the river.

The taniwha noticed Pearly too and said, "Good morning, Pearly. Why aren't you at school?"

"I'm not going to school any more," she said, "because my feet are far too big. Every time I stretch them out they trip the children over."

"But they're magnificent feet," he said. "I wish I had feet like that. I can only crawl with mine but I could walk with yours."

"I think they're terrible feet," she said, "and the children do too."

"I'll soon fix that," he said.

"Why, what will you do?" she asked.

"You leave it to me," the monster said, crawling a little closer. "Now all you do is change feet with me and then they'll all be sorry. They'll reach the stage where they'll like your feet, if not even love them."

"I don't think so," said Pearly.

"Not that there's anything wrong with my own feet," he said. "Mine also are magnificent. But they'll all still be sorry."

He crawled up out of the water and swayed upon the bank. He was a very large monster with eyes like moons and a mouth like a cave in the cliff; and his tail was long and ridged with spikes and swept out over the water. Waves ran this way and ripped out that way to break on the farther shore. "Good gracious me," remarked an eel, "is this a storm coming?"

Pearly looked at the monster's feet. "What dreadful feet," she said. "Very much bigger than mine. Big long toes with claws at the end and covered with ugly scales. Mine are better than that."

"You don't like my feet?" said the taniwha.

"They frighten me," she said.

"That's just it," said the taniwha, "they'll frighten the others too. What some people want is a jolly good fright to teach them a lasting lesson. Some people don't appreciate what they've got. Right? Now you unscrew your feet from your legs and I'll unscrew mine and we'll change feet for a day."

"I'm glad you said 'for a day,' " she said. "I wouldn't like yours for long."

"Neither would I like yours for long. They are far too small."

"How lovely," she said, "to hear my feet called far too small. I feel better about it already. But your feet have got only three toes each. I've got five each on mine."

"Extravagance," said the monster. "I can do all I want with three."

"But you've got four feet," Pearly said. "I've got only two."

"That's your misfortune," the taniwha said. "I don't know how you manage. How can you crawl, let alone swim, with only two feet? It's better being a monster."

"Which two will you change with?" Pearly asked. "Your front two or your back?"

"Oh, the back two. I should say. I want to have a go at walking. My front two are really hands. Would you like to change hands with me?"

"Oh no, I'll keep my hands," she said. "Nobody hates my hands."

The monster unscrewed his two back feet, Pearly unscrewed hers and in no time they had changed. The taniwha didn't look so impressive with a girl's two feet at the back. "How can I swim with these," he said, "let alone crawl?"

But Pearly looked awful with the monster's feet, not like a girl at all. She could hardly keep her balance and soon she had to crawl. Even then the claws got tangled up among the river grasses. "How can I walk with these," she said, "let alone run?"

"I don't think I'll last long with these," he said. "We'd better change back soon."

"And I won't last long with these," she said. "We'll have to change back soon."

"I'll meet you after school," he said.

"After school," said Pearly.

Off walked the taniwha into the water looking so very silly, and off crawled Pearly up to school looking even worse. She didn't like her face so close to the ground and her eyes were filled with dust. She'd far rather walk. As it was she didn't get up to school till well after playtime when the children were doing their spelling.

"Look at Pearly's feet!" Bernard shrieked, and dashed behind the door.

"Look at her feet!" Tiny squealed, and dived beneath the table.

"What dreadful feet!" screamed the children and fled off out of reach—some in the corners, some in the porch and some up in the rafters. Even the teacher trembled. "Where did you get those feet?" she cried. "You didn't have those before!"

"I changed with the taniwha," Pearly said, sitting at her desk.

"What for?" asked the teacher.

"Because," she said. She stuck them out in front of her and started on her spelling.

"They're covered in scales," the children said, "and they've got long claws. And they've only got three toes each and they're very much too big."

"They're out of all proportion," said the teacher.

Pearly stopped her spelling and began to cry, and everyone else did too. "But why did you change them?" the teacher asked, coming a little nearer.

"Because," repeated Pearly.

"You changed because we didn't like the feet you had before."

Pearly cried louder and all the others too. "I can't even walk with them," she said, "let alone run."

"We're sorry," wept the children, "for what we said about your feet being big. Your own feet were pretty. They were the smallest we've ever seen."

"Whenever I noticed your feet," said the teacher, "I always had the feeling, what slender feet."

Pearly began drying her eyes. "He said he would make you sorry," she said and went on with her spelling.

Just at that moment what should happen but a strange knock on the door, and who should appear but the taniwha covered in wet from the river. But he wasn't crawling any more. He stood upright on Pearly's feet looking very silly, and you could see his underbelly which he was always shy about, and he held his front feet across to cover it up, blushing like anything.

"There are my feet," Pearly cried, "all covered in mud from the river!"

"You can have your feet," the monster said. "I can't wait till after school. You know what is wrong with these feet of yours? They're far too small. I can't crawl any more, and as for swim . . . I nearly drowned. I've had enough of Pearly's feet and I want to change back this minute."

Pearly put down her pencil and stopped doing her spelling. "For heaven's sake!" she whispered.

"Hurray!" cried the children but they didn't rush back from all their hiding places; they all stayed where they were. They watched the monster change feet with Pearly, and before you could say "Claw!" each had his own again.

"That's the finish," the monster said, "of changing feet with girls. I'll never do that again. That comes of being sympathetic and trying to help people. I always knew I was soft. My ideas run away with me and the next thing I'm in trouble. You should have seen me at the bottom of the river trying to crawl about; all the eels were laughing at me. It was sheer hell." He crawled about angrily on his feet.

"And another thing," he said. "I couldn't hang on to a single thing with only two claws. When Andrew's uncle tried to drown himself because Andrew's mother didn't love him I couldn't get hold of the man. He got away from me and climbed out of the river and went back to the dance hall. Oh, what a loss! As fine a meal as I've ever missed."

He crawled about on the floor, relieved, his tail sweeping the walls. Down came the pictures the children had made and the piano flipped through the window. "Oh, what beautiful feet I've got! There are no feet like them. Never will I part with my feet again, whoever cries by the river. Well I'm off home. If I don't remove myself at once I might swallow the lot of you. It's only my soft heart that's saving you, and that's for sure," he said. And off he crawled away down the steps leaving mud and water behind him.

Pearly was overjoyed, and so was everyone else. The children came back from their hiding places and gathered about Pearly. "Hasn't she got wonderful feet," they said. "The very smallest ever."

Pearly sat down in her desk again and tucked her feet under, and as for the others they sat down too and all went on with their spelling.

August 10 · When K had gone to Home Guard I put Jean Humphrey's Iceland poppies which were wilting by now and dropping their petals . . . I put them in the fire—the flowers she had not brought up herself, that had come by a strange hand, that had carried no written message—and tipped out the used water. Through the quiet kitchen it diffused a smell of death . . . the death of love and friendship. I pushed the last sour-smelling stalks into the grate, thinking, "Lilies that fester smell far worse than weeds." Then crossing to the window I opened it and the shining rain came in. After which I had a game of cards with my girl who now is a radiant being, almost frightening with that "intense love" that Freud attributes to children in his *Introductory Lectures*. Then when she was asleep I settled to my book, and struggling with the thought therein, I came upon the revelation that the breaking of the thing between Jean and myself had been the result of some failure within me rather than within her, some shadowy shapeless violence that wrecked the sensitive balance of intimacy. Obviously I could not keep my head in the career of emotion, could not "with quick alternate vision" see beyond infatuation and that while I "raved on the heights," did not "behold the wide plain where our persistent self pauses and awaits us."

I thought back over the year to Jean across the road, to a

distant remark of hers: "No, I don't know you, Sylvia. I don't know you."

"H'm," I had replied, "well, well. We'll have to arrange a showdown one evening."

· · ·

These last few nights I have been studying Jean's books of collected poetry, soon to be returned since she has enlisted—every chosen verse, pointed or flat, original or clichéd, until it came home to me with what remarkable persistence I had thrown back in her face an overboiling generosity. It has been as much as I could do not to run down across the road to her and apologize; but even I know that what has gone cannot be recaptured and that the best thing to do is to let it lie—even before I read Robin Hyde's "Division":

> If it were nothing but some deep abyss
> Opened between us—
> I should have faith: and parting would have end—
> I think our feet would cross on rainbow, friend.
>
> But there is more to conquer—all that long
> Pageant of ghosts, in stained and tattered dress—
> The swift mistaken word; the unmeant wrong;
> The pride, grown harsh at last for loneliness.

After which, not without relief, I recorded the error of my loving outside the family at all and felt ready for Jean to go off to war. There remains only that little matter of my return to the plain where my "persistent self" should have paused and should be awaiting me.

October · A young doctor, we hear, who wants to do a thesis on T.B. among the Maoris, is taking over the nurse's cottage across the road. Now what makes a man want that, I wonder? It is a very wide area up, down and across the river and reaching to outlying towns but it remains no more than a nurse's job. He won't stay long, that's for sure.

We've had my mother up for a week. I said to her, "I'm glad you confessed to K that you were responsible for making me like this."

She was baking some marvelous scones. "Oh, I told him a few things in the garden this morning."

"What did he say?"

"He said he was afraid your teaching would make you grow away from the home."

Grow away from the home . . . had I ever grown into it? But I kept that to myself.

November 12 · In the middle of my yellow jaundice the new doctor is brought into the bedroom, at which I put on a magnificent show of being a bright patient, making little of my ill. He turned out to be soothing and courteous and, even more than Nurse Jean Humphrey, *poised*. Wonder of wonders, he has asked us *all* down to the cottage *in writing* and gives every evidence of liking to come up. He nursed me through the "yellow peril" with a thoroughness and gentleness that equaled Jean's when I had grown-up mumps and that I thought could only be found in a woman and that stirred in me the old desirous secrets on the theme of mothering that has been imbedded in me ever since the Coast.

November 14 · Have been raving tired for the last three weeks since the yellow j. and have been obliged to go to bed straight after tea each night. Dr. Mada has not yet got used to my staying three quarters of an hour, no more, returning about eight or before. Actually no one so far of the medical

world who has lived in the cottage has been able to understand
that with some people there are other things to do besides talking in the evening. I purposely avoid seeing too much of him
anyway. I'm too weak emotionally to risk leaning on anyone
now. My first duty to myself is to be independent, but it's far
from easy at the moment, for the new occupant of the nurse's
cottage is courteous and satisfying and impressively cultivated. Anyway I haven't got over Jean yet.

November 18 · Friedmann didn't play last night as announced,
I wonder why.

I practice in the dark now on the piano. I always did for
that matter but now that I know Dr. Mada prefers music in
the dark I do so with an added purpose.

There was a school committee meeting in the school last
week and the Maoris came in after supper. Old Matenga made
a lovely Maori speech of appreciation to us to which K replied
in English and I in Maori.

November 22 · We had a most successful War Institute meeting on Wednesday, six Europeans and three Maoris. A happy,
gay and profitable time during which Dr. Mada spoke on first
aid to us. He's a wonderful substitute for Jean. I whispered to
him at afternoon tea, "Do mix with the Maoris."

"Oh, I forgot," and came among them.

I can't believe that here I am loving someone again immedi-
ately after my vows to the contrary but it is so and I can only
excuse myself in two ways: that I must have been made precisely *for* loving and that, in the casual way of miracle, Dr.
Mada is probably the one person left in the world who could
inspire it again. It is beyond my comprehension of the coinci-
dental and I can only record it . . . that with the entire
world to choose from he should live across the road from me.

But I think that even if I never again play to him in the darkness with him sitting silent and still in the wicker chair with no clumsy comment at the end but only a "Thank you," I should be able to take it. Anyone who survived the Coast should be able to take anything. That's if I did survive it.

December 15 · A few Mondays ago I went down to see Saul Mada after sundown, bare backed, barefooted, white shorts, in the warmth of the evening, ostensibly to take him the milk from our cow but really to see him again after his TB trip to town. And there he was in his garden trying to burn a heap of twitch grass and other assorted weeds to the lilting music from his radio, that gay little prelude from Bach—which sounded so sweet on the softened air that as I approached his gate with the billy I improvised a simple dance.

"Hail," I heard. Which is my word and I wondered that he used it. I danced sedately down his path until I paused before him.

"Go on," he said, "go on."

But I was shy.

"Go on," he repeated.

Take the silence and be damned to you.

"Go on. Is that the sword dance?"

"No, the billy dance."

"The *billet doux?*"

But I settled down by the pile of grass he was trying to burn.

"Do you like sitting by bonfires?"

"Yes."

Then in a pacifying stroking voice he began telling me easily all he had done in Whanganui, about booking in a TB at the chest ward, about the TB specialist, Dr. Howard, about the Maori children he had taken to Dr. Howard keeping him waiting on the way in *and* after the film they went to, until he finally ended up, "Well, that's my day. Now tell me yours."

"I've had a beautiful day. Oh, I know—I must tell you about Sister Hobbs. She greeted me, 'So you're still surviving here, Mrs. Henderson?' And I said, 'I *live* here, Miss Hobbs.' She came into school with that smile on. That particular kind of smile which that particular kind of person puts on . . . you know? Sort of professional."

"Christian," he corrected.

"That's it! A Christian smile."

We talked and laughed on beside his recalcitrant heap of weeds as the darkness came down until inevitably the conversation veered round to ourselves. I said, "What did you bring home from town? Something really unpardonable?"

"Nothing out of a bottle so disperse your hopes at once."

"Why?"

"No money. As simple as that."

"Oh. Why didn't you ask me or something?"

"And I'm not likely to bring any more home for a long time."

"Why not?"

"There isn't the need."

"Do you mean to say that you are not going to bring home any more lager at all?"

"Not for a good while anyway. Money shouldn't go on beer when we don't need it."

"And I have to rely on the forest rangers for my lager now?"

"You shouldn't be drinking at all as you very well know. You're the kind of person that shouldn't, says the doctor to the patient."

"Why shouldn't I?"

"Because it's a stimulant."

"To think that I have to rely on what the rangers save from their orgies. K brought me home just *one* last night after Sunday's blowout."

"Oh, I think it's so silly to be dependent on beer as they are. There must be something more to life."

"Don't you be too sure. You're looking at the rangers from your standpoint. Not from theirs."

"Oh well—" he turned some coals with the pitchfork—"I suppose everyone has a right to their own lives . . . to live their own way."

"I don't believe in an even life, like that," cigarette demonstration. "You should go up and down like this," cigarette lurches and dips in the twilight, "touch the peaks of inebriation."

He poked at the coals. "But there have got to be some people like me to keep the world stable while the rest of you go up and down. There have got to be some drawers of water and hewers of wood."

"It's you that says it."

"Do you really depend on lager as much as that?"

I surveyed my bare legs on the darkening grass. The dew was settling on us. " 'To see me as I am, have thou the strength. And even as thou art I dare behold thee.' "

"You confess very gracefully."

"You are the kind of man who should drink beer."

"Why? So you'll have someone to drink with?"

"Don't be so obvious."

"I'm sorry."

Pause.

"There's no apologies on the River," I said.

He settled down on the evening grass beside me. "What is the reason, then, that I should drink?"

"Well, firstly, since I am the kind of person who shouldn't drink, then it follows logically that you, being the opposite of me, must be the kind of person who should."

He turned his dark eyes to the silhouette of the treetops against the sky. "Well, at a stretch, you might call that a reason."

"We could arrange it to be a reason," at which we both laughed.

"So, come on," he urged, "what are the other reasons? One, two, three, four, five, six . . . ?"

I thought warily. It's dark, I thought. I'm liable to say something I would not in the light. I too looked up at the patch of sunset sky above the treed horizon. "As for other reasons—" and was aware of him turning his face toward me in the embracing darkness— " 'and even as thou art I dare *not* behold thee.' "

He received it in silence, then got up professionally. "Come on. You must come in out of the damp."

"Oh! You've suddenly turned into a doctor." But I got up and moved down the path with him. "Otherwise you'd be all right."

Saul lit the fire and made coffee and passed it to me, waiting on me respectfully in a way that touched me in a place that was hidden and something awoke that had never seen daylight. I received the cup, then the cigarette from his tending hands, with a pride that was agonied in its newness, agonied at the splitting and breaking open of covers never before opened. I didn't recognize our mutual age. This new thing . . . a father? No. I felt he was my mother, the thing I had demanded from Jean. A young man of my own age—a mother?

I dived into his German art book, the enormous weight of it on my bare legs while he moved the lamp behind the couch, sat near the gramophone to change the records of the piano concerto, then I lay on the rug by the fire, and he didn't appear to care that I saw his face uplifted, hand over eyes; didn't seem to mind revealing his inner self in the enchantment of music, revealing that music to him was such that he didn't want the light. As he changed the record the first time I ventured to say, "I don't know what your life is like."

" 'Neutral-tinted haps and hazards . . .' " blowing out smoke. He passed me the cigarette box, lit both mine and his and when the second movement was over he said, "I don't know what yours is like."

I didn't answer.

"What was that verse you spoke outside—the rest of it?"

" 'We mocked the careful shieldings of the wise, And . . .' " Pause.

"Go on."

I spoke the next line prophetically. " 'And only utter truth can be between us.' "

From where he sat above me I felt the turn of his head as he looked down upon me during the crashing of the third movement.

When I left at about nine-thirty we went laughing up the night path together, the two of us full of banter, and he pulled me to walk on the grass. "Isn't this lovely on bare feet," he said.

We parted at his gate laughing like anything. K laughed when I told him all this in the morning. Indeed as spring finally bloomed into summer on the River we all laughed a good deal, at home or at school, until Pearl Harbor.

January 4, 1942 · Deep in the oblivious Christmas holidays. A benign Saturday afternoon yesterday. I was walking with the little ones along the forest road, exploring as usual, and we came upon a deserted whare. Set well back in a paddock where the trees had been cleared here was this ramshackle unpainted weather-thrashed cottage where no one lived at all. On the instant I went mad on the place. I saw it for what it was: a place of silence and peace for me—no voices, no banging doors, no pace, no rivaling passions face to face and no war either. "I could have this place," to the children, "to study in and learn to write!"

"Why doesn't someone live here?"

"Someone did live here once."

Not locked. Three rooms. A big one in the front with high sloped ceiling, a low-roofed kitchen at the back and, leading from it, a bedroom of doll's-house proportions. At the back door a sort of little porch, a little yard also with a Walt Disney fence. "This is mine, this is mine!" to the children.

January 5 · My sister Pauline has arrived from the capital where her home is between three targets just asking for Japanese bombs, but her baby has been sick with new "klums" and my baby has too. Last night, although reeling tired from nursing I went with K through the blackest rain to the Store to get the mail, a thing I never do, not only because I know he needs me but because I myself need him, however it appears to the contrary. I'm mad on the man and love to be near him, I ask no more than that . . . even if it means tripping over rough loose metal in the darkest and wettest of nights.

When we came home we found Dr. Saul there attending Pauline's baby, with my baby making most of the thunder bawling from sympathy in my bed. K at once picked up Pauline's baby, whose father had been lost in Greece and who finds comfort in men, while I strode past Saul to Dannie, and when K said after a while, "Saul is going now, dear," I stayed with Dannie and murmured "All right."

· · ·

The next morning when Pauline went to Raetihi with Dr. Saul Mada to get her hair done I took the opportunity to devote myself to K, it still being school holidays, caring for and wooing him back after neglecting him lately, until in the afternoon when I was sitting on the step, a breather from nursing the babies, and watching the rain, he came up behind me and kissed me on the back of the neck, and when I went to bed with my darling at night we read before we loved.

. . .

I can't bear to see Saul unhappy. The faintest disharmony rankles unbearably so that in answer to my heart but against my judgment I ran down this morning and found him in the back garden. Casually he turned, "Hullo."

"Hullo . . ."

He turned an indifferent spade.

"Perhaps I shouldn't have come in the morning. I should come in the afternoon."

"I won't be here this afternoon."

"Oooh."

"What have you been thinking this morning?"

"About how much I love you."

"Well, I really must go."

"Go? Where?"

"To my work. I've got a lot to do this morning. Finish the garden, clean the car, enter charts and go round the village in the afternoon."

"Have a cigarette, Saul. Why are you different? Why don't you like me?"

"I haven't said so."

"You haven't *said* so."

"Well I haven't indicated it."

"You are different."

"It must be my work that makes me different."

"I shouldn't have interrupted you. I shouldn't have." Suddenly I run. Back through the cottage, along the path, across the road, and don't stop running till I hit the hill, which is a matter of slogging and puffing.

. . .

I must get on with my writing. My work has the failing of going down before emotional upheavals as it did when Jean was here, and it goes down before illness too, physical illness as well as the illness of love. And I've been loving dangerously since I came to the River even with my anti-loving resolutions still pale green. Without doubt I'm a weak-minded person.

What I need is a place of quiet to work in. It turns out that the whare up the road is on land leased from the Maoris by Mr. Snowdon, and I'm told that no Maori would ever live here again and that it is called Suicide Cottage. And I'd better get going before the Japs arrive. For the first time in our history we know what it is to have the enemy threatening our homeland, let alone with our division on the other side of the world, which could be a good thing, because as the Japs swept down the Asian continent the Australians lost fifteen thousand troops in the Malayan debacle and two thousand in Java. The Japs struck their first blow in our immediate area on January 4 when they bombed Rabaul. The next without doubt will be on this river, bang on the top of this hill.

·II·

February 3 · Today, Tuesday morning, two days after the
bombing of Timor, the February of our second year on the
River, we all started school again from the head of the house
to the baby. We didn't know what for with the enemy so near
and with most of our troops in Egypt. But it's lovely starting
school on the first school day especially with us all together.
No one left at home.

It does impress me that when you are geared for work, even
though there's much more to be done and less time to do it,
more is achieved than when there's plenty of time. My own
carefully prepared and ruthless program is running well so
far: study from four-thirty to six, children and breakfast till
eight, music from eight-fifteen to nine after the children have
gone to school, put in a big day at school till three, some large
project after school like a preserving pan of jam to be bottled
by six, prepared during the day by Pauline, the whole program balancing on bed at nine to be early at my books in the
morning again. Which means no Saul in the evening, of
course, but that in its context could be a good thing; pleasure,
like work, responds to discipline.

I'm frankly thrilled about school these days and take hot
pride in my room, so bright and light with the painted desks
worked on during the holidays. On the wall are paintings by

the children, the duster and chalk boxes focuses of color, the number road painted on the floor a constant mecca for children where they learn to count and add by games—or I mean them to—while high on the back wall, after weeks at the top of a ladder during the vacation, my large wide chalk picture of the Pied Piper overhanging all.

Naturally, it's raining, tremendously so on hills, forest and river, but oh, you get used to that. For one thing it supplies a glamorous backdrop to our happiness at school and to our interest there. If only there were no war . . .

·   ·   ·

As I have said, even pleasure responds to discipline. It was Saul who came to me one morning, in his brown eyes that magnetism, that something darkly intensified. "Come down today," he whispered.

I put plates on the table for lunch. "I'm glad you asked. I was waiting to be asked."

"Oh no, Sylvia. Come down whenever you want to."

"I can't." Two cups and saucers on the table. "I might interrupt your work. I mustn't do that again."

"Good gracious!" He stepped back. "It wasn't as obvious as all that, was it?"

I picked up my books for school. "I really mustn't interrupt you again."

"Come this afternoon. Come to tea."

"I can't promise."

By afternoon it was thunderstorming but out I ran into it barefoot down the path to his door where he greeted me passionately, "You look so lovely. I'm so glad to see you." I lit a cigarette and said, "I'll take ten minutes off for this."

February 11 · None of this foreboding about the war, the sinking of our troopships, the slaughter, failures and defeats both near and in the Mediterranean, the pages of casualty lists in the press and the possibility of K being called up . . . none of it impairs our absorption at school. On goes the Infant material painting, sawing, printing, hammering and drawing. It remains a sad fact that all this in time may be for the Japs, but not a deterring fact. At the moment it is here, whereas the Japs are not . . . at least not yet.

I continue teaching the senior girls housecraft over at the residence, showing them in particular the intricacies of making tea as well as how to serve it, since no Maori housekeeper of mine yet has realized what it means to K and me to be passed a cup of tea when we return from school. Naturally I begin on Hellen, whose unconquerable latecoming in no way diminishes her charm—a big, full and dark-skinned Maori with the blackest of Maori eyes. And don't forget those white teeth when she smiles, which is every hour of the day.

And I go on standing Pearly beside me day after day practicing the sentence, "Mummie, give me a handkerchief for school," until today after a clear two weeks the impossible actually happened: Mummie *did* give her a handkerchief for school, although what that's got to do with the war effort so far escapes me.

And I go on trying to find out how to teach. I plan so carefully, so fully prepare, meaning to forestall failure, but so often it falls through. I've got the desks in a single half-moon round the long room with an open area in the middle like a Maori marae* with me strutting round like the Maori chief. They look so pretty all sitting there in this orderly half-circle, their black heads over their books . . . or not. To see it is to think it's a lovely school and I an excellent teacher, but I do wear uneasily the uniform of the Supreme Commander for I'm not that at heart, though I need to be. After all some-

* Marae: an area in front of a Maori meetinghouse where speeches are given.

body's got to be in control; that's what I'm paid for.

Perhaps I care too much about the appearance of the thing. They all look so nice, and the room looks so nice with its generous areas of color. But with my increasing study in the early morning I am more and more inclined to wonder if it looks as nice inside. All the books I study are about the *inside*. I should know more about the inside and I have picked up a bit. When I'm teaching formal number and reading I'm well aware that the children are concerned with something else, or some of them are. If only I came across some passage in a book about how to relate the outside to the inside when at work teaching children; there was a book at training college about that very thing, Rousseau, I think. It was . . . I remember writing an essay about it and winning top marks. Something not in accordance with the syllabus where the outside and the inside became one thing, reciprocally inspiring.

Or, more significant, so that they and I became one thing like being married to a man . . . I no longer being the Supreme Commander. It's often one long battle against the energy of their alienated feeling. Back on the Coast I'd been getting somewhere, I think, far from the haunts of inspectors, out of range of the Education Department—out of reach of criticism. I even taught the Maori language there . . . O heresy! But here, with roads and bridges and no tidal rivers, an inspector could walk in any day.

"Please, Olga's got a fit."

I look up from my table where I've been pondering and there's Olga on the floor, smiling and her eyes rolling. "Does she bite her tongue or anything like that?"

"Sno."

The nice half-moon is spoiled. A few leave their desks to cluster round Olga and forget about their sums which I had prepared so precisely. As the time goes by with Olga's fit, I know that when I look back upon the day I'll see that I've missed again. In anxiety I get up and go to her, concerned for my program rather than for Olga. "Olga," I order, "stop having a fit."

"Please," from Tiny, "Olga she can' stop having the fit." A sort of subordinate officer in spite of her flimsiness.

"What do they do at home when she gets them?"

"Please her mother she throw the cold water on Olga."

"Oh, I couldn't do that." The minutes tumble by, the number lesson should be over, and I should be at the table marking their work. "What makes her get them," I ask. "Why doesn't the doctor give her something?"

"Please she's spelled."

"What does that mean?"

"Please," from Jacob, "Olga's got an evil spirit in her. It's trying to get out, the evil spirit."

"How did it get in?"

"Please Olga she walked on tapu ground. Olga walked on the graves by Mrs. Hira's place and the evil spirit hopped in her."

"Shess."

"Shess."

"Please Mrs. Hira she got the evil spirit in Mrs. Hira."

"What, did one hop in her too?"

"Please yes. Mrs. Hira she live too near the graveyard, Mrs. Hira."

"Is that why she's sick?"

"Shess."

"Well I go sometimes to see Mrs. Hira and if that's all graveyard there I've walked on graves too. But I don't know of any evil spirit that hopped into me."

"You're only a pakeha," said Jacob. "The evil spirit doesn't enter a pakeha."

I look down upon Olga more concerned now about her than about my program. A thin little girl with bare feet and an overlong dress handed down from some older girl, straight black hair hacked off round her ears any old way to economize on the combing. She's settling a bit now but still she smiles. "If an evil spirit hops in so easily you'd think it could hop out again just as well."

"Pleaseno."

"Sno."

"Well, why doesn't somebody try to get it out?"

Jacob replies, "Mrs. Henderson, Mando's mother is good at chants but she doesn't know this one. Her grandmother knew it but she didn't teach it to Mando's mother before she died. So nobody round here knows it now. My grandfather said it is just as well."

"Please," from Pearly, "a big evil spirit it live in Suicide Cottage."

"What?"

"Shess. In the Suicide Cottage."

"How do you know?"

"Please the evil spirit in Suicide Cottage it make Whistle and Mai Mai die there."

"Is that why nobody lives in Suicide Cottage?"

"Shess. The big evil spirit it live there, the big evil spirit."

"And you're quite sure it doesn't hop in the pakeha?"

"Please the evil spirit it don' hop in the pakeha, the evil spirit."

As for the orderly, pleasant-looking half-circle of children with their black heads down . . . where is it? Wrecked, the entire number lesson I'd planned so industriously, so hopefully.

The few times when I have achieved unity with them have been in the stories I have told them arisen from what they have told me about the river, the taniwha, eels, feet, love affairs in the pa and evil spirits, and strange to say those stories were curative, if not actively creative. Not exactly the stories themselves, but the accidental fusion of their minds and mine: Jacob has never forgotten his book since, no one teases Pearly about her feet and she herself keeps them well tucked under. Accord . . . rapport—that's the magic. Something, some benign power, is born from rapport, however brief. But no story of mine, I'm sure, could ever coax the evil spirit from Olga, should I attempt one. Surely Saul has a sedative or something. No, his supplies are short in wartime.

With a charming smile Olga gets up from the floor and looks about at the children in inquiry. "Where you-fulla been?" she asks. "You-fulla been away?" At which they laugh like anything.

As I make the effort to return to my table to see if there's any number lesson to mark I think about creative rapport, not only between the outside and the inside of a child, between them and me, but of the fusions, or lack of them, in my own life: the absence of accord between warring facets of myself, between myself and the world. Accord within a girl would mean integration, which in turn would make a worthwhile person.

"Bring up your work, Tiny. Jacob, give your little brother some chalk and a blackboard. Look after the little chap." They laugh at that too.

.   .   .

Fitted into the overall program of the home, the preparation of food for the winter goes on with exciting success (war and Japs regardless, and the possibility that we'll have to take to the forest) except for the potatoes having the blight, although we have saved the main crop with spraying. The hay for Susie the cow is in the shed, the garden is progressing as well as it can in the nonstop rain, and we're up to our fifth preserving pan of jam. But the battle for Singapore has begun so the enemy is close. Maori Ada down the lane is reputed to be making a Japanese flag to welcome the Japs when they come, which could point to at least one of the reasons why the Home Guard has not been issued rifles.

As for the evacuees from the capital, we can't stand them more than a week, they can't stand the rain for more than a week, nor the unfamiliar isolation, so they catch the bus back again. Except Pauline and baby although, "There are times, Sylv," she said, "when I honestly would prefer the three targets round my home to all this rain and mud."

As for the book I'm trying to write, it is me, but *I am K*. I am his wife and to be a worthwhile wife I need successful expression. Everything is for him: the happiness of the children, the smooth running of the home, and it is for his sake that I have so severely reorganized my program after the pandemonium of Saul's arrival. Indeed, even the joy I share on occasion with Saul . . . that's for K also.

February 14 · Yesterday what should happen but this! Mr. Snowdon called in at the school and gave me permission to use Suicide Cottage a mile up the road through the forest for as long as he possesses it. Not the large front room where he stores farm gear, docking and fencing tools and such, but the little kitchen at the back where the fireplace is. Pauline and I have already cleaned it out and after school today K is going up to work on it while I mind the children. True, the tragedy room leads off this kitchen but the whole thing is *terribly thrilling!*

Saul calls it That Awful Place but he could still bring himself to fumigate it, as if any medical person could fumigate away the presences of those two young phantoms. "You're mad," he said, firmly fumigating. "Daft."

I hated these words and I'll punish him later but at the moment he was fumigating. "I can still feel them in that room," I said. "In mind I see them plainly, Whistle and Mai Mai, lying on the bed in their blood. Does it weigh on you, Saul?"

"No. I feel only how wonderful it was that there should have been such a love, that there *could* have been . . . to make any two people do it."

Because, I reflected secretly, you have felt so far only the wonder of love and not yet the sorrow. "I feel," I said, "only the edge of the pain that could make two people do it."

"Yes," he considered it thoughtfully, then again, "Yes."

"That was the night of the soul," I said, "from which they did not return."

Carefully and professionally Saul sealed another crack in the wall. "I'd like to know the night," he said, "but I would return."

My Jonquil, who was with us, said, "Mummie, Pearly said that Whistle and Mai Mai died here because there was an evil spirit here, Mummie. Is that true?"

Hastily, "No, it isn't."

Saul said, "It's certainly a place for the night of the soul."

"It's all soul-morning to me."

February 16 · It is a matter of note that after the years on the Coast the friendships I make harbor heartache. It seems I cannot love moderately or even singly, and I look for a mother in men and women the moment they reveal a regard. On the Coast I sought a great sea-rocking mother in the indifferent ocean who never rocked me. Moreover, being always over-avid, I demand from those I love a love equal to mine, which, being balanced people, they cannot supply. If only my neighbors across the road so far had not been a succession of medical people whose life's profession was Looking After, and if only I were not the grand look-after-ee of all time . . . the thing's fantastic. Yet when K came back from Home Guard in the evening he managed to mother me, pulling me into his bed. "You mustn't cry like that," he said.

But I cried much more before I'd finished telling him of the misery in myself, and as always he told me he loved me, adding that he had been often lonely since Dr. Mada came. "I accept it," he said. "It's normal and innocent but I'm still lonely because you've always been so dependent on me. Now I feel your need of me has been transferred. Gone."

"I'll stop anything that comes between us."

"There's no need to stop anything. All I want is to know whether, when you come back from the cottage, you are not just waiting to go back again."

Which was so near the actual case a little time ago that I was hard put to deny it. "Whatever I am is for you. If I find happiness over the road, then that too is for you." At which he smiled, I think. "It's you I need and love. I love you so dearly. You are my life."

. . .

"Give me that truck, Frannie," from Dannie.

"No."

"Give it to me, I say!"

"No."

"Do you want me to cry!"

"Yes."

"Oh . . ."

March 2 · A new Monday in March: I'm here at the whare and I'm terribly happy! O Life, the silence, the enrapturing silence! No . . . not wholly. There's a mason bee here I'll have to dismiss. Only room for one builder here. Surely he can work outside as the cicada does. Outside the cicada sounds happy enough, no more than part of the sun.

I'm lovingly conscious of the roughness of it—yet there are still some things to be done. I wonder if I'll leave these walls unlined and the floor uncovered. That spare wallpaper at home I'll paste on the ceiling to hide the old newspaper and the pattern of the mason bees. And I really must get K to push the iron of that chimney straight . . . that great big hole in the side . . . and in time I'll see to the hearth. And I might bring up in my haversack a patched green curtain, when Saul brings the windowpane from Whanganui, and K can make me a table to replace this packing case. He can make it with the dressed timber that Wingo brought when he came back from the mill, and when Pauline gets her furniture from Wellington, I'll be in the position to bring my camp stretcher for relaxation at times . . . and a rug and some sort of cushion. "You need to have something to lie on," Saul said, viewing the thing professionally.

Through the small window that K has restored, the same treed range we see from home, across the gully the sheep whitely dotting the hill and the deep green gorge. Nearer still on the slope the thistles, and right close the Disney fence. Silence . . .

Yet the cicada is loud and certain, the intermittent mason bee, the usual tui, the baa of the sheep and the flies cruising in and out. Silence? I cannot mean absence of sound, and now I know just what I mean: no voices and no doors banging. No pace, no demand for answers. No "Does-he-love-me, does-he-not?" and no war news. No room of children on my hands sharp with responsibility, no fits from Olga, no tears from Pearly or revolt from Jacob Rau. Think of the rests I could have up here. Think . . . think, O Heaven!

Silence. "The silence where man has been, self-conscious and alone."

A recurring memory this afternoon with a day of school behind me is of the pressure within to do something, and indeed the need to do it, of the starts and attempts I've made in the past—even on the Coast!—and now finally *here*. Settled in this crude little heaven really doing it.

I wonder if the Japs will let me or whether this whare is

destined for Maori evacuees as K believes it is—this residue of living I have cleaned and adored, that Saul has fumigated, that Pauline and Jonquil have helped me to paper, that I have scrubbed three times so far, with the lock that K has put on the door and the window he has restored—or whether my work is to be once more put aside forcibly by an intent other than my own, postponed this time till the Japs have been, until they have gone again . . . K maimed or dead, the children starved, changed or dead, and my own life made so ghastly by their coming that I couldn't learn to write, given any silence . . . maybe I myself may be incapacitated or killed . . . or whether the years unfold ahead full of peace and work.

The two clear thoughts lie side by side: the nightmare and the dream.

March 4 · When are the marauders coming? We were sitting at breakfast with K. "Oh," I said, "I wish we could get on to this cave-digging. I wish we had a store of food in the ground."

"Oh," from Pauline, "I'll dig and I'll dig and I'll dig. Can't we start tomorrow?"

"We'll make it where none of the Maoris know."

"It will have to be out of bawling range."

For a fleeting moment I saw the children's beautiful faces pleading for food as Pauline went on, "We'll dig a cave up the valley a bit, in reach of water. No Japanese order can stop water running, not here anyway."

"I dreamt," I told them, "that they came and that I was one of their advisers. I was showing them round the valley. I'd rather stay in the house, I think—keep in with them. I'd do anything for the children. I'd go on their side for the children."

K said, "Before you went over to their side, we'd shoot the children."

"But you said I wasn't to shoot the children."

"A light breakfast row," from Pauline, "on whether or not to shoot the children."

We started right there on collecting the apples with Pauline up the tree and it touched me to see how happy she was reaching for the glossy fruits and passing them to K. Such a relief that K enjoys her company . . . if only he enjoyed Saul's as much.

Although things have been going better lately. This weekend has been one of my high places with both men loving me at the same time . . . a rare condition. In fact K and I have been lyrically happy week after week. Those nervous attacks were plainly the result, not so much of overwork, but of the strain of my love for two people pulling different ways. It must be . . . since it is only when I see them friendly that the strain lifts, as it did last Saturday night as I set off down the hill when K called gaily, "Give my regards to Saul." In any case I do seem to be making headway against my unpopular habit of vanishing across the road. Praise God for willpower.

I'm not denying of course that Saul was away for two days, that I felt his absence, and that before he went he said, "We'll have to start a correspondence on Thursday," because he was to bring a visitor back with him—but whatever the reason I did stay home.

"I liked your letter," he said as I passed on the way to Suicide Cottage.

"The part about what you mean to me?"

"Yes."

"I've known that for a long time."

"How long?"

"Months."

"Months?"

"Don't you believe me?"

"Not wholly."

"It's true."

"Is it?"

I looked at his dark eyes,

"Oh, Sylvia. It makes me want to do things. Get up early and work."

And on the way back from the cottage when I ran into him putting the car away he said, "When I think of you I . . . I . . ."

March 10 · I'm here again in the whare eight days after last time. Five-thirty in the afternoon after a day at school, with K minding the children.

During the centuries of the golden prophets, well before Christ, when the Hebrews sang psalms all day the priest at times would call a pause to give the psalmists a rest, and the word he used was "Selah." A Hebrew word. In charcoal and lipstick I wrote this word "Selah" on my door.

March 11 · Today too I came here after school to Selah at half past five after preparing the evening meal. I came so joy-fully the wild wet mile to get my quota of work, not to men-tion the necessary ration of silence, but owing to the pane of glass Saul brought still not being in I ran into a bout of the old frustration. All settled down, fire and everything, slippers on, books spread out, when a wind-chased shower plunged in wetting all my things. I can't move my table away as it is nailed to the wall and the floor, too.

So an hour went by while I collected water in the teapot from the dripping roof to make paste in a former paint tin to stick paper over the hole of the window, but the wind wouldn't have this, nor the rain either. So I finally gave up any idea of writing what I had planned coming up, wading up the road through the rain. These few lines I'm entering with a board across the gap.

Moreover I'm sick and vomity, more so than I've been for a

week, which could be another pregnancy, and also with Saul gone to Whanganui again my heart has a list to it. There are four battalions in action today: those of the mother, the woman, the artist and the weather. Who will win I don't know. The orders from the commander of the Home Guard on Sunday were "No surrender." My orders from myself to myself are also "No surrender."

I know that K cannot take too serious an interest in Selah, my haven, since he is only doing it up for evacuees, but is it likely that any Maori, however pursued by Japs, would risk so much as one night in the whare with the ghosts of two young lovers, not to mention the evil spirit? They'd settle for a year with the Japs first. But I wish he would do the window. In any case the thought of giving up my window, however gaping and wet . . . that would be truly war.

At least our design of life till Jap time still holds: to make all necessary preparations, take all precautions but live on regardless—teach at school, train our children and my work at Selah; our daily life. Preserve continuity till the very last roadblock.

Yet beneath all this—wet window, enemy and nausea—something still beats. Today I brought the wallpaper for the ceiling in my haversack and the oversize orange cardigan to leave here, which already adds a touch of comfort, and next time I'll bring a sack for the hearth rather than buy one for refugees.

Silence. A different kind of silence today of shrill wind and rain. For this first time I note the rain-wraiths hurrying down-river between the misted forests, and the gale spurts through the hole in the cartoon chimney in a way I had not foreseen when it was fine and calm. It prowls round the room like an evil man, like a cold influence of hate on the soul, and the sound of it outside is like the offstage effects whenever a thriller is broadcast, grossly overdone. Or could that whistling and groaning mean the return of the lovers? Rather a Jap than the return of the lovers.

I'll return through the rain to K now before the twilight comes, and go to bed early. I do need you and love you, K.

March 12 · This afternoon there was Saul on a chair in the school where he had found me at study, and I sitting on the table, and he was still hurled about with passion. "You," he was saying, "you smell so lovely." And there in me were the petals opening all over again until the conclusions I had come to at Selah lately battled their way to the surface. I intercept the reaching hands, at which, with infinite gentleness, love and regret, he withdraws them saying, "Is this part of the new order?"

"Dear, I have been a faithful wife under the circumstances."

"You've been wonderful."

"I mean to remain a faithful wife."

"All right. The motion is: You remain a faithful wife."

"I need your help. I'm a very weak-minded person."

"You're not."

"I am."

"Right. I'll take over the censorship again now that I know what's required."

. . .

It is true that I have been dangerously in love with Saul this year.

. . .

It is of no real moment that Saul should say I am wonderful, having known me less than a year; it would be another thing if K said so, he having lived with me nearly ten. I brought this up at teatime to which he answered, "The trouble was with our early married life. You were up here," hand raised high, "and I was down there," hand below table level.

"And now you're up there and I'm down here," hand groveling on the floor.

"No, no," both hands level, "we're both here."

"Oh no. You're up there and . . ."

"No, no . . ."

"Oh yes, I'm usually the one in disgrace now."

"You're not always in disgrace, dear."

"What I want to know is, what sort of a person am I to live with? You ought to know. It's what *you* say that I care about."

"Well . . . you have so many talents."

"Leave the talents out of it. They have nothing to do with the sort of person one is."

"Well, you're a very worthwhile person."

Not wonderful. "That's all I want to know."

I must correct Saul.

In bed, however, he laid his hand on my head. "You're a clever lamb. I'm proud of my lamb. I knew what I was doing when I married you."

"You're my father, mother, family and future. As well as my love."

March 13 · For the third time this week I'm here after school at Selah but I got away earlier today. At half past three I made it. Twenty minutes to walk up bringing water from the creek, ten minutes to set the fire, sweep room, wash hands, change into slippers and then get out my books. Absolutely *thrilling*.

Alone up here in the mysterious hills robed in their evergreen, in my quiet crude room, I reflected on the effects of the war. Far from being impeded, our work has intensified, as if caught up in the global energy, while Pauline is inspired by something gleaming beyond the death of her husband, a home for herself and the baby and a new life. Indeed all of us at this time of threat—excepting Saul alone, who, thinking and reacting differently from us, remains unimpressed—are too busy to see the danger; in spite of rather than because of it our thought plunges deeper.

March 15 · Sunday is my own day at Selah but I didn't do any work on the book, spending the day fixing things with the family here. K built a bed frame against the wall from old timber he found outside and I nailed the sacking on it. He finished the table with the smooth dressed timber that Wingo brought from the mill, Jonquil filled the nail holes with putty, fixed up a box for an extra chair and helped me paper the cupboard inside, white, where I put the food, all with the two boy babies consistently under our feet. And because I was sicker and more vomity than ever, paying this time for *not* being pregnant, I worked harder than ever. This program I have set myself, or rather that has set itself upon me like an invisible aggressor, this pace at which I live: wife, mother, lover, teacher and what I call my "work" . . . well, no Jap could drive me harder.

Yet I believe that rather than harm me the routine will spruce me up, and from my study as I go along toward my obscure goal—to be a worthwhile person—I learn things that confirm it, and from experience, too. Do the word study at home in the early morning but leave essays and drafting for Selah; in fact leave anything creative at all for the silence of Selah.

March 16 · On Monday in school I feel so happy after a Sunday at Selah, bringing cheerfulness with me as though I'd had a drink of something, of hope, and at once, alarmingly and pathetically, the children pick up this mood of mine second-hand and have it for their own. To start with, we do a lot of loud singing with me letting fly on the piano all about the King's horses, the King's men, they marched up the hill and they marched down again, and a song about Did you see the leaves fall softly, softly, down, down, down? so that Jacob's little brother Ihaka is profoundly impressed with school. "Is he really five?" I ask K.

"So they say."

"He's very small," I tell Jacob's grandfather, who turned out to be a preacher of the Anglican Church, as he sits in school with Ihaka between his knees.

"Him come up by-m-by." He demonstrates with a hand. His English is not as good as the children's though no doubt he is fluent in Maori, so the grandchildren's English—Mary, Rebecca, Jacob and Ihaka's—must have come from the parents in their seclusion across the river.

The thing about small Ihaka is the size of his mouth which would do credit to a young taniwha, and as he sang this morning full out you could see halfway into his belly. Conceivably, a trip on the boat to Whanganui for school clothes small enough for Ihaka drew a blank, but they bought him clothes regardless of size which he wears regardless, all brand new: trousers near his ankles, socks near his thighs, boots lapping under his knees, and a jersey like a maternity dress, but this boy is very happy. We should sing much more if for him alone.

A comforting acquaintance, hope, a contagious thing like spring, inebriating like lager. The room takes on new colors that I didn't organize myself; it is hope that deepens the hues of their pictures on the wall, brightens the painted desks, duster and chalk boxes and inspires the late autumn roses that Rosie brought from the House to glow with romance, and it is hope that makes them laugh so loudly to see Ihaka singing. Were we allowed we'd sing all day and end up with a party.

"Well, children—" I rise with reluctance—"we'd better get on with our work."

"Please we haven sung Pussy Willow."

"That's a spring song and it's autumn now. Come on, back to your desks."

Tiny is back, since she's an orderly girl and likes doing her work, but there's a whole lot of dawdling and foot-twisting and disappointed faces. "Please sing a autumn song."

"Shess! Shess!"

"We've sung it. Come on now. Back to work."

"Please teach another autumn song."

"Please yes, plis yes, plishess, shess."

"What if I don't know another autumn song?"

"Please you know those hundred songs."

True. "Look, there's Tiny started on her spelling already. All of you get going on your words and if you do them well, good writing, none wrong and no talking, I'll remember another autumn song."

Flash . . . they're all at work. Funny thing, obedience, the way it works or the way it doesn't work, but they shouldn't need bribing surely. Were I a good teacher there would have been in the first place less wildness in the singing, fewer songs anyway and more control of myself and them, so that when it came time to work they would have gone to it without a bribe. I've got a terrible lot to learn that never cropped up in training college, not least how to keep emotion out of teaching; I suppose a teacher should be able to turn off emotion the moment it is out of place, which it seems to be in a classroom, but I'd have to learn how to turn it off in myself first and is that possible? If it were possible I'd live in much less tumult.

I sit on my chair before them, accessible. The only one left not at his work is the infinitesimal Ihaka, who doesn't know what to do. "Ihaka," I say, "you come to me and have a little read."

"I can't read," in a strange deep voice.

"Never mind, I'll teach you. Here's the book. Come up by me, Ihaka."

He doesn't. He stands there lost in his clothes.

"Jacob, bring your little brother to me."

Jacob brings the clothes to me deep within which is to be seen, if you look closely, Ihaka's threepenny-bit face, and he stands warily at my knee. "See this picture, Ihaka? What's that?"

"Dunno."

"That's a train. Haven't you ever seen a train?"

"Please no."

Heavens . . . here's the "please" from the very start! "Ihaka, you say, 'No, Mrs. Henderson.'"

"No M's Hen'son."

"Mrs."

"Mrs," he follows.

"Henderson."

"Henderson," no trouble.

"Mrs. Henderson."

"Mrs. Henderson," quite well spoken.

Now say, 'No, Mrs. Henderson.'"

"No Mrs. Henderson."

"That's very good for a little boy," at which the whole class laughs for nothing. "You're cleverer than all the big ones. They don't call me by my name, they call me Please. Now, little boy, have you seen a train?"

"Pl-pl . . . no Mrs.—" pause—"Hen*der*son."

"See?" to the others. "He's a clever boy. He calls me by my name."

Andrew, the son of Wingo, with the same smashingly handsome face, "Please I can say No M's Hen'son."

"You've just said Please."

A chorus of laughing from the rest of them and fast blushing of Wingo's Andrew, then an outbreak of "No Mrs. Hen*der*sons" all over the room, so that I stand to hold them down. "Not so much noise, children, you'll disturb the other room."

"Please," from Bernard, "we're as clever as Ihaka."

The others accuse, "He said Please!"

"Shess," I answer.

Not so much energetic laughter, but a little. No one has to be a wit to make Maori children laugh who laugh for anything at all or nothing, and usually with surprise, which after all is an ingredient of wit, surprise. "You know what, children?" I say. "Instead of my name you call me Please, so I'm going to call you Please. That's fair." I address Tiny, "Please, when you've written your words get somebody to hear you spell them."

"Shess . . . no-no! Sh—yes, Mrs. Hen*der*son."

Bernard makes a concentrated effort. "Mrs. Hen*der*son, I've finished my words. I'll hear Tiny hers." But he's a white boy with a language lead on the Maoris.

"All right, Bernard, you hear Tiny."

From Tiny again, "Please and I hear Bernard his?"

"Shess."

Confusion. She starts again, "Please," stops, pauses, thinks, prepares then, "Shall I hear Bernard his, Mrs. Hen-*der*-son?"

"Yes, Tiny." The others admire her.

I turn back to the small boy beside me. "Now then, have you seen a train, Ihaka?"

"No Mrs. Hen-*der*-son."

"Well, that picture is of a train. People have a ride in it. It goes by itself like a truck but it isn't a truck. It's like a long long mail car with a lot of seats and it makes a very big noise and it can carry fifty people. The mail car can't carry fifty people. And it doesn't go on the road because it has its own road, all to itself. See that word beside it? That word is 'train.' Can you say 'train'?"

"Train," from the clothes.

"T-r-a-i-n. Spell it like that."

He does, clearly.

"Now I'll see if you can write it."

"I can't write it."

"You might be able to. You bring me your blackboard and chalk and duster." But he remains where he is.

"Jacob, bring your little brother his blackboard and chalk and duster, please."

A shame. With his twice-daily trips across the river in Grampitty's canoe he should be trying to write "canoe," but when Jacob has brought his things he sits on the floor at my feet and says unexpectedly, "I can write train," and the next thing he has written quite a good word except that it is not "train." What is this word? I look closer. It is "canoe." Then he forgets all about me and draws a canoe with the family sitting in it.

Now where am I? Something I don't follow here. Something about the inside not mixing, not the same as the outside, about the inside defeating the outside, having more power. About the known being stronger than the unknown, which so far is no secret since way back on the Coast we used the vocabulary of our environment. The whole of the first book that children start on is a mass of carefully chosen unknowns, bed, can, train and such . . . at least it is for the Maoris. Unlucky to be Maori even in a Maori school. Sitting, thinking, in a baffled way, I hear them spelling their words with zest and fun and barrages of laughter but that doesn't come from the books they read, it's still supplied from the spring of cheerfulness that I brought here this morning.

"Andrew, do you know all your words?"

"Please I . . . pl-pl . . . no Mrs. Henderson. I can't spell aeroplane."

"Have you ever seen an aeroplane, Andrew?"

"Pl-pl . . . no Mrs. Henderson."

"You said you would teach us another autumn song," from Eva.

Let me see . . . What was that about a nut in a tree? A little brown baby, a nut, balancing up in the tree, but there are no nuts on the trees here. Another of these imposed English songs, just like the King's horses and the King's men. Unlucky really to be a Maori when it comes to education. But before the bell goes for playtime, with their spelling done well, their books away and everything picked up from the floor:

A little brown baby, round and wee,
With kind winds to rock him sat up on a tree . . .

On account of Ihaka I got near to something this morning, a stubborn secret, about the inside and the outside of a child related or unrelated in his reading. But I don't know the secret and it's not in a book.

My baby Dannie runs in and climbs on my knee. "When you are bigger, dear love, I'll teach you to read."

"I'ne two, I can read."

"Can you? What can you read?"

" 'Course I can read the cocoa."

He's just had a mug of cocoa outside along with all the others. Behind these lovely blue eyes he got from his father there must still be a picture of this large white mug with the red-brown cocoa in it.

March 20 · Five A.M. again . . . exhilarating! All this was over while I minded the baby when Pauline went to Wellington, but she is back now, having taken out a fire-war insurance against her furniture and brought here her linen and husband's clothes, and cleaned out her flat. It is ten days since I've been to Selah, to work, I mean.

·   ·   ·

Yesterday morning when I was a playing a march for the children to come in I heard K's voice behind me unexpectedly. "I'd miss . . ." he began, but I jumped, at which he moved away.

"Go on, dear!"

Again he came. "I'd miss it very much if you didn't come to school now." Was it because I had slipped on making my usual call in his room when I first came over? Oh eternal man!

. . .

By now we have had several visitors at school and are getting the idea we exist, seldom having seen a visitor on the Coast except a rare inspector and a rarer district nurse who would ride out on horseback between high tides and dreadfully ride back again. Now—health officials, locals and guests from the House short of somewhere to go have found somewhere to go, and I turn on school like a concert. When Saul called in at playtime some guests were examining the Pied Piper high above on the wall. "I'm glad you came," I told them later. "I need appreciation." But neither Saul nor I spoke of my many carvings and drawings on banks about the valley and in the silt of the river bank. Why bother anyway? Nothing lasts long in the rain. Neither does chalk last, even not in the rain; my favorite media have no future.

. . .

During this same day three mysterious men called at school, one an Army captain, assessing the capacity of the school to accommodate extra children with a view to establishing an alien camp at the House. When they'd gone we sent for Pauline— "Major news!" and closed the door.

"Keith, you're called up!"

"No," we laughed.

"Somebody's going to have a baby . . ."

"We wouldn't be laughing like this if we were."

When we told her she cried excitedly, "I'll be able to live a life!"

"I think," I added later, "that it'll be the Japs assessing the accommodation for dozens of little Japs." I looked out at the rain, which I love. "Although actually, if they knew how much it rained here . . ."

"They'll have the rainfall on their maps, surely."

· · ·

I could have gone to Selah after school with Pauline home again, but I didn't. There seemed to be a deeply hidden thread running through the day uncovered by my recent brush with pregnancy which was also uppermost in Pauline's "Somebody's going to have a baby . . ." It brought the men I love closer to me, and me to them. Which can always be fulfilled with my husband but denied damagingly for the other . . . the source of our constant quarreling, the unacknowledged source. Damaging for Saul rather than me . . . conceivably. The thought that my ruling feeling for him is some spirititually filial thing rather than a man-woman thing . . . to try to tell a man of thirty-odd that I want him to be my mother . . . Poor Saul, to run into this abnormality, this heart-breaking no-exit. As for preening myself on my excellent morality, my magnificently faithful wifehood against the fiercest of persistent temptation . . . I couldn't tell myself such lies.

So I didn't go to Selah after school. I went out into the rain to gather flowers for Saul when he returned. I gathered all the white flowers as a symbol of the truth we're often examining . . . at least I think that when I start. White cosmos round the house and three white roses before I went up the road for the thousand-jacket growing on the banks, which I see on my way to Selah, some little white roadside violets tucked in the fern and white flax from his own garden, all of which I set in a big bowl of his on the table in his room. An arresting startling show. Beautiful to the point of trembling passion but without the flesh to receive it.

March 22 · Five days since I've come to Selah. I got comprehensively wet this morning in the heavy rain, for as there

had been barely a drizzle when I left home I had brought no
hat; then down it came. A precious half-hour slid by in
battle with the fire, and while the water boiled for tea and
my coat hung to dry I lay on the bed and thought, Ten
days since I've actually worked at Selah, at my books I
mean, although I have pulled off a few quick trips to complete preparations. But I should be under way by now. Saul
brought the glass from Whanganui, and although it is not
yet in, the window is repaired and curtained in green, if
only a patched-up cloth. I have on the floor unpicked wool-
sacks, on the bed a quilt of sugarbag and sheeps' wool I made
years ago and an old dear cushion. Clean, plain and rough but
heaven haven to me.

Then with tea and a smoke I got going on an idea that was
pushing about to be seen . . .

Saul said he would call in on his way home from his
rounds, at which Selah assumes a new value as a place where
a conversation is not obliged to battle for its very existence,
and at five o'clock I did hear through the torrent on the roof
the hum of his car and from my door I saw it slipping away
in the rain but although I had made some minor preparations
to welcome him I found myself working on a design for living in the heat of which the disappointment failed to endure.
It involved the conflict between the way a man lives and the
way he is meant to live in accordance with nature, in which
case he needs to know nature. Which is what I call truth,
this correspondence of a man's ways with those of nature;
this thing Saul and I have been tussling with lately.

Truth has beauty, power and necessity. "Truth is the
greatest of all blessings. Without it man is blind," from
Rousseau. "It is the eye of reason." Yet Krishnamurti said,
"Truth is a pathless land and no one can lead you to it."
From which my own Selah-bred design arose this afternoon:
Acquire knowledge to learn of truth. Maybe that is why I

put those flowers in his room, if in fact truth is white. Half the time it's red and black to me with lightning flashes through it.

I sat over this till dusk caught me out, a time to be absent in a house of spirits. I lit a candle and made a paper hat. Nor was I nervous getting away as I often am in the haunted half-light, but felt lighthearted walking home, lighthearted in the rain.

When I reached home and walked in dripping from the night into all this warmth and light I found K getting ready to go to Saul's Red Cross lecture in the village hall. He had bathed the children and put them to bed and the whole three were happy. Tomorrow morning I plan to make an especially nice breakfast for Pauline for being companionable to K, talking and listening at teatime when I'm away. If Pauline never lifted one hand in the house her conversation justifies everything.

· · ·

On Sunday evening with the children in bed and Pauline writing letters I talked to K about the design. "The intellect is the tool to find the truth. It's a matter of sharpening it. Since I've been studying I'm much keener-witted. That's one reason I'm learning to milk the cow. I'm going to take over your afternoon's work sometimes and you can have the time for more study. I can chop wood and feed the fowls. We'll share the time."

"I can't possibly allow you to do rough work, chop wood and do the fowls. Not when you have the desire and the ability and the opportunity to do what you do."

I was surprised to hear this.

He continued, "What I thought two months ago and what I think now are two different things. I've tried to be broader about your going away. People who can do the work you do should be allowed to do it and those who can't should hew the wood and draw the water, feed the fowls, chop the wood and milk Susie."

This distressed me.

He went on, "There's no need for you to take on my afternoon work."

"But my work loses its value unless you are happy. Everything loses its value. Your contentment comes before my work."

"I'm happy."

"No you're not."

He looked at me with interest. I went on, "You're not getting as much time for study as I am. You're the real mother of this family; I'm just one of the children. We must share the time."

He pushed the kettle over the flames. "But your study means more to you than mine does to me."

"I question it. But in any case that's not my point. Your work means more to me than my own does to me because your work involves your contentment and that comes before my work with me."

He was interested but looked doubtful.

"It's the truth," I added. "Unless you are happy in your work mine is valueless to me."

K examined my face as though he was seeing it for the first time.

"It may not be apparent," I said, "but I love you and you come first in the world with me, before everything, before anybody. You and the children. My family and home are more to me than my work. If it came to the choice it would be my work that went overboard. No doubt I've appeared to be a failure in the home but that is not indicative. Do you feel I've failed you in the home?" I called on all my courage to ask this question which could draw a devastating answer.

He put out two cups and saucers. "Well, it has crossed my mind that you shouldn't have married."

Catastrophe! "But I've been a good mother! Look at me all through my babies. How I stuck to them on the Coast."

"Yes. But what I mean is that a person, any person, with your inclinations should not marry. You should have gone on with your work. Marriage has sidetracked you."

Desperately on the defensive, "I wash and dress the little boys in the morning, and Jonquil. I feed them."

"I know. What I mean is that people like you with talents and ideas should be undisturbed by marriage."

"Ah . . . but you see! I wouldn't have had these desires at all if I hadn't married. When I didn't teach and had no babies I hardly lifted a brush. Hardly did a thing. The *need* to study, to do, to make, to think, *arises* from being married. I need to be married to work."

He poured the boiling water on the tea. "I still think that you should be allowed your work in preference to my being allowed mine. Your desire is stronger than mine."

"That's quite possible. But I'm still going to hurry up and learn to milk Susie and take over your jobs sometimes."

We had tea, ran off the dishes and went to bed. Neither of us lowered the flag, neither won, and we haven't talked about that since, but the part about his coming before my work must have registered and held for there's been a tenderness in his manner toward me like the reappearance of the sun, and that close feeling has returned.

March 24 · As it happened, when K had to dash off without notice to his ailing father I did take on his jobs and loved it. Wore his sou'wester in the rain and his enormous gum boots, fed his fowls and chopped all the wood, cared for the sitting hen and fed the cat. Pauline and Ruth (the Maori housekeeper) did the inside work. I stripped the pear tree from a ladder and with a saw, bottled eight large bottles of pears and stored the rest . . . although I've got to admit that Mando milked Susie.

March 25 · This March found the Japs at Singapore, then at Timor, then they took Java . . . racing toward New Zealand. Yet we are less concerned about this than we were about Pearl Harbor, when we really sat up and took the war seriously. My word, did we gather up our soldiers then, extend medical services, boost the Air Force and such. Even a Home Guard.

Never did we get over that shock of Pearl Harbor, yet with the Japs practically wiping their boots on the doormat of the country we are inclined to be casual. Go on planning our year's work at school, creating a colorful number scheme, teaching our own small children music and speech in the morning and storing our year's food against some hypothetical siege; we build a huge crate under the trees on Sundays for all this surplus fruit as though this year would turn out all right, and if we do stop to wonder if any of this is worth it, we keep on anyway from sheer force of habit, keep on keeping on regardless. K is a master of Keeping On Regardless.

Besides by operating regardless you dwell on and draw precarious comfort from the more acceptible alternative that America will stop the Japs, that she physically *can*. Also there is no doubt that familiarity with the sense of danger does lull one to blindness, so on goes this concentrated year.

I'm not saying I'm not deeply haunted by the thought that K may have to go sooner or later. New age groups for the ballot so far haven't done their worst, but I remember that during the First World War we got past the men with three children. Or I remember my mother saying it. Between the pace of school, home and my attempts to study I feel the thought under the mind that I'd known all along he would go . . . all along. Since the war began, when we were on the Coast, I've heard myself clearly thinking, This will return to me when he's gone, and I'll remember when he's overseas.

.   .   .

Sunday afternoon at Selah. I'd planned a full day's work from morning on, but a 3 A.M. session with the babies, started by Pauline's who wakes more at night since her father was killed in Greece and followed up enthusiastically by my own baby . . . this session ruined my day. I've got here but I'm sleepy. Yet I did salvage some joy bringing water from the spring, gathering wood for the week and lunching gloriously alone on tomatoes, peaches, radishes, apple, banana, biscuit and chocolate. I'm inclined to think that eating is a private thing and should be done alone, like other bodily functions— you don't see animals sharing a meal. After which I rested on the bed and dozed for an hour, the heaven unscratched, un-matched.

Saul still calls it That Awful Place but it remains Selah to me; the hours spent here whether working or resting are a pause from the high battle of life. Although I am very sleepy today I am still very happy and mean to continue with my design. From its rough condensed shape at present I'll compose some practical formula to use through the life ahead so that I may end up somewhere sometime a sort of "worthwhile per-son" . . . before Saul and Pauline and the baby arrive for a cup of tea.

March 31 · The last day of March, and Saul thirty-four. Whether by chance or design . . . more likely chance . . . Saul had one of his routine health inspections at school this morning and a talk to the children on it, but it is frankly by design that I lunched at the cottage between twelve and one with Saul—a staggering affair unrelated to health. As much as

I could do to climb that hill back to school at one.

But to give him a party at That Awful Place takes all the chance and design at hand, forethought and planning, not wholly for the occasion itself, but to get there at all in the harvesting season, to extricate myself from windfalls and apple jelly, bottling and such, you've no idea. After school I dashed off at three leaving the tearful little ones behind, a drastic cost the doctor never pays—and Saul arrived serene at five, his black hair elegantly parted. "Everyone," he said, forgetting his term That Awful Place and that he had called me daft when I had first conceived it, "should have a place like this. Everyone should have two houses. Children should have a house of their own."

I was startled. That would be the solution of Jonquil. I was silent.

He went on, full of his new thirty-four years, "If I had a kid I would build it a house of its own where it could do exactly what it liked."

"But a child's house of its own is the wide outside accessible to it at any time. Anywhere away from its parents. They really do have their own existence on occasion."

He didn't reply, but put his mother's birthday cake on the table.

I threw my butt in the fire. "The idea is a good one. Brilliant."

But Saul is a master of no replies.

Then among the clustering ghosts we got going on this cake and the sherry I'd brought in my haversack, and smokes, after which he stretched out on the bed while I sat on the stool by a fire which blazed like a fairy tale. "Is this heaven," I asked, "or isn't it?"

"It's nearly here," stretched his limbs luxuriously, "oh, it's here all right."

"Unadulterated."

"Unprolificated."

From his back he lifted his glass, "To us."

"To nothing happening here in Selah."

"To the baker of the cake," from him.

"To heaven."

The ominous rain on the roof . . . "Only utter truth can be between us."

"Have you been to heaven lately?" I asked.

"Do you mean since I've been away from you?"

"No. I mean in the last few months."

A very long pause, then a very soft "Yes." And I knew he meant last Saturday night with all that music and lager. Then he sat up.

"I love you terribly."

Tears . . . mine.

"It is incredible that there should be anyone in the world as beautiful and as wonderful as you. Darling." He stood. "I love you." He came. "My dearest love." He was at my knees. "Darling, darling Sylvia. I love you."

"How long will you love me for?"

"Ever."

"How do you know?"

"I don't know it. I feel it."

"Saul . . . I'm weak. Nothing must happen in Selah."

"You're not weak."

"We are squandering this love," I said. "We should use it."

"No. We're not squandering it. We've had it for three whole months and we're still in love."

"It's not that. It's that we're not using it. We should only have times like this as a reward when either of us has achieved something. Something in our work."

"Yes."

"We could meet again when we've finished the books we're reading."

"I've nearly finished *Scorched Earth*."

"How much more?"

"Three chapters."

"But that book's heavy going."

"Yes it is. But you should read it, darling. It's . . ."

"No, no . . . I'm not going to read it."

"Yes you should."

"No I shouldn't. It's not in my line."

"Of course it is. It's in everyone's line. It's all about the history of Asia."

"I know it's good but it's not in my line."

"What do you mean—your line?" Settled back on the sack.

"My design then."

"What is your design?"

I told him.

"I thought," he said, "it would be a kind of five-, ten- or twenty-year plan."

"A design is not a plan."

"It is."

"No. A plan would nail you down act by act, govern you year by year. But a design—" I lifted my hands—"is a matter of shape. Some wonderful shape into which can be fitted any experience at all whenever it chances to happen. The thing is . . . to get going is to know oneself and what we can of the truth."

"And can any ordinary mortal," sincerely, "hope to learn to know himself on his inadequate own?"

"*Anyone* can do *anything* if he has the urge!"

"And if there is no urge?"

Impatiently, "Oh, we can't supply *urge*. It's either there or not."

He got up, went to the table and filled the glasses. Distantly, "How is the work going?"

"Thrillingly."

"I'm jealous."

"I thought you would be."

"What are you reading?"

"Why?"

"It's another way of asking when we'll meet like this again."
Passed me my glass.

"Well . . . when I've finished *Antic Hay*, then."

"How far have you got?"

"About halfway." I smiled. "He's suddenly quite interested in my reading."

He strolled back to the fire. "It's your turn to call a toast."

My toast—secret toast—is to our parting. Easier than this never-ending denial, the inhuman agony of it, the quarrels. "I've got a toast but I can't call it."

Swung round, "Tell me, tell me!"

"No."

"Why can't you tell me?"

"Because if I do something will happen in Selah and nothing must happen in Selah. You know I've told you before that I want Selah to be a place of peace where nothing ever happens to me."

"I promise nothing will happen here. Just tell me and I'll remain the same."

In the agony of passion I reached to touch him but he stepped away. "Look!" I cried out. "Something is happening here. You've stepped away from me!"

" 'And only utter truth can be between us.' " He stood still with his eyes shut.

"What are you thinking?"

"Nothing."

"What are you feeling then?"

"Nothing." Standing motionless in his dark-brown birthday clothes, his black hair parted elegantly, his eyes still shut. A still, pathetic figure with closed eyes in the growing gloom of a haunted whare. Stepped away from me, with his eyes shut. I thought, no one standing beside you. How greatly I love you.

As we cleared up he didn't speak and as we walked back along the road through the forest he sang, determined conscious singing. Neither did I speak, being in no mind to put up a show that I didn't feel. At our two gates I remarked, "I can't think of anything appropriate to say so I'll just walk off." Which I did. K was sweet and kind to me as he always is now since I told him he meant more to me than my work. The loving harmony between us now.

Saul sent me flowers the next morning before he fled downriver on his rounds—with a new verse he had written attached. A candid verse which I richly deserved. But the flowers were a stunning scarlet bouquet with one white stock in the middle, his own symbol of the "utter truth." A far better reading than my all-white gatherings.

At school my teaching was bad, and the children worse. That any circumstance whatever should have the right . . . *have the right*, that's the dreadful part . . . to intrude on my inner thoughts, hack at my inner feeling, at my memory of Saul the night before. Had I not been teaching I would have sat for an entire day, still, on the arm of a chair, dwelling on it, pondering, recalling, working out why this, why that, he said this, then I said that, and then . . . living it all over again. That's the sin—their intrusion on my mind.

Poor work, wrong spelling, noisy interchange, my bad temper, didn't put their books away before playtime or lunchtime, and somebody started Pearly off crying in that shrill unstoppable way—that devil Andrew, I think. I didn't notice the books on the floor until after they had gone, dusters and a lot of chalk. Wretches. As for singing happily together—never.

Until the evening as I write here with the babies asleep and K at the Store where the telephone is, ringing up town on Home Guard business. This homicidal intrusion of one upon the other—that's what my teaching is most of the time, especially the reading, intrusion upon their inner thoughts and feelings, but *I* do it every day, every school hour of every school day, and it's the pain that makes them naughty.

·III·

April 1 · April Fool's Day is a day that one should mark on the calendar and underline severely, but this time we forgot. There's much to do fast in the morning but when we got to school just in time, Mando turned up and sent me down to the village on an April Fool's errand to see Mrs. Hira who wasn't dying at all, K to old Te Koau on some trumped-up story, and Saul miles downriver to a cock-and-bull patient. We all went, too, unsuspecting, but for the last time.

April 9 · Last night K brought home from the Store some exciting mail—our grading. K did very well, much better than me—conceivably. And news of the visit of the senior inspector. Not to mention Saul's brother, a big name from the education world—a letter from him saying these fine things about our school, about the Pied Piper and the number scheme, asking for more information about both. Thrilling, really. It gave me an embryonic idea that I had something in me of the teacher after all.

After these two letters I'm flat out getting more drawings put up in the porch since we've completely used the inside. We drew beautiful pictures of books yesterday, quite convincing. Even Saul said they were and K said it was the most arresting drawing he had seen from children. How I love praise!

Yet these recurring flames of rejuvenation, regeneration, do not always survive the war effects concentrating about us. A common thing to hear now, "When you go into camp . . ." and new words enter our vernacular: "torpedo-bomb," "mortally wounded," "destroyer," "survivors," "Japanese power," "carriers," "cool efficiency, relentless action, determination and superb heroism"—not all new, but used in a personal context. I wonder again and again just what I'm doing for the war apart from the presidency of the Women's War Institute and the regular wretched war euchres. Could there be some less obvious way of relating? A more obvious way of relating my work with young children to the wholesale slaughter in these parts? If there were, I'd work it. I think, however, that the link lies somewhere in the area of the violence waiting in the undermind, lapping in the undermind . . . but I haven't got the equipment to see it.

A strange silence in the playground at lunchtime today. Where have they gone? No sight or sound of a child, whereas they usually play loudly after lunch. At the blackboard where I'm putting up work I pause. Have the . . . have the . . . ? I stroll in next door to K. "Have the Japs come or something?"

Running steps in the porch, it's Bernard. "Please sir the boys are fighting."

"Who?"

"Please Holly and Shally."

"Where?"

"Down the hill on the road outside the school gate."

K gets up from his table and goes out the door with Bernard trotting behind and I return to my blackboard. It's against the rules to fight at school but now and again they do, sometimes the boys but as often the girls, with a different technique.

Holly and Shallcrass are Harry Rowe's sons and they have

fought before, brother to brother. Harry Rowe is a Maori who married a white wife, so that Holly is dark with European features and Shallcrass is as blue-eyed and golden-haired as a son of our own. Racial conflict within the family.

Holly is the younger and fatally handsome, so that both Jacob's big sisters are in love with him, Mere and Harriet, and of course Caroline has always an eye for a profile and it's easy enough to follow, I'm attracted myself. He's not only got this face but this hot personality, a combination of irresistible magnets. He cries out loud when he's hurt sometimes, which makes him more appealing than ever, and he screams when his brother teases him—and although Shallcrass is bigger and broader than Holly, the younger will attack him like an animal at bay, to the point of stones and blood. A wonderful free show for the rest of them and as a rule no one tells, but then Bernard is a notorious tell-tit.

I know what will happen any time now: you'll feel rather than hear the children returning up the steep steps from the gate, silent-tongued and silent-footed, and you'll hear Holly's passionate sobbing, then the tap running outside where someone is washing his blood off, after which the two boys will be brought inside by a bodyguard of other boys to have it out with the headmaster while the rest of them flock in the porch and under the windows to listen for the canings, all in orderly and respectful silence, respectful to the play of passions. After all of which they'll disperse, the voices will lift again and the laughter, as though nothing had happened at all—the only register of the show is K, who is upset when the children fight. Except that he doesn't thrash them when they fight—as did the former headmaster who was a retired soldier, they said, from India—but tries to bring them round to reconciliation.

Harry Rowe's white wife lives in town but Harry has kept the boys, eleven and twelve years old, and seems to be ambitious for them, talking of scholarships and college from time to time. I believe the house where they live is wonderful to see with no woman in it. Clothes meet you at the door, Saul said, on the beds, behind the beds and under the beds, all over the table and chairs and heaped high in the corners, unwashed clothes with no one to wash them . . . Holly says he has fifty-nine socks. They buy more clothes when the ones they've got are too dirty to wear, and it is said there are shoes there by the dozens although the three of them go barefoot. Harry Rowe looks revolting walking round the village with his dirty bare feet and the cuffs of his long trousers trailing on the ground. I suppose he works sometimes but he's always at hand for any scandal in the village, talking his heart out, his mind, soul and stomach out. Talk . . . Harry Rowe! He'd talk to the Japs, were there no one else. He'd defeat them with his tongue alone. Plausible, too. We avoid Harry when we can but he comes up sometimes to see about the boys. Actually he's clever but has no disciplines, and he is biracial interpreter in these parts, his face a picture of rapture amid the waves of words.

Yes, I feel the return of the children up the steep steps from the gate and I hear Holly's sobs. Yes, and there's the water running, Holly's blood flowing, and K comes in: "If there's any way of preventing an older brother teasing a younger brother, then I don't know it. My brother teased me like that unmercifully."

"I hate a bully."

"Shallcrass is not a bully. He's gentle in the playground, but somehow when it comes to his younger brother . . . Why must it be this way?"

"Our Frannie teases Dannie, you know. Three teasing two."

"I wouldn't think twice about putting a bully over a desk and giving him six of the best, but Shallcrass is not a bully."

I'd like Holly to come inside to me, he being upset and no mother to comfort him, but I know he won't, of course. Teacher is teacher and pupil is pupil and never the twain shall meet, but I expect Mere and Harriet are with him, their slim fingers tending, and no doubt Caroline in the wings fingering her black silk plaits.

This violence lapping in the undermind, exploding at times where the crust is thin. There's some link between this among the children and the daily death of thousands in the war at our door but I haven't the equipment nor the perspicuity to put my finger on it.

April 10 · Into April now and well into autumn with the Japs well into the South Pacific. Exactly what is happening? No secrets come over the radio or into the New Zealand press.

On Thursday I lost my Selah key again and Digger Wallop's roving brother Toby, who was having a beer at our place after school, said he had seen it in the whare door, which I had reason to doubt. But I let him drive me and the children up there to find out and I gave him a glass of sherry. The key was not there, of course; he had his own reasons for wanting to come up. "Why," he opened, "leave a lovely home to come up here?"

"Peace . . . from the front line down there. From my children and everyone else's."

"Everybody says you come up here to meet Tom Snowdon."

"*Do* they *really?*"

"Yeah," sipping the sherry, assessing my reaction.

"Well, I like them old too, but not over about . . . let me see . . ." thinking of a gray head I love, "not over fifty."

"But Tom told me himself that he was as good as the young ones yet."

"I expect so." I preferred the Wingo scandal with his youth and good looks to this latest—my name being linked with Wingo's just because Ada had found us drinking beer alone in her front room, whereas all that happened was that Wingo was telling me about his white girl at the House called Undine. "Sylvia, this is not beer talk. I love that lanky tart at the House. I'd marry this tart, ay, if her parents would let me. I got a wife I know, and I got that waster boy Andrew. The parents they say, 'Wingo he won't work for Undine. He won't make a home and stick to her.' Sylvia . . . I will work for Undine and I make a home and stick to her. I love that tart. This no beer talk."

"What about Undine, Wingo?"

"Undine she say, 'No another man for me. Only Wingo for always, ay. Only Wingo I marry. My parents they don't let me marry my Wingo then I run away. Wingo, I go to live with my Wingo, for ever and ever.'"

"And what about Andrew?"

"Undine she say, 'I take Andrew. I be a mother for Andrew.'"

Then Ada came weaving in covered in cosmetics, and the next thing here's this scandal. But I preferred that to this with Tom Snowdon, a gray-haired middle-aged man whose wife left him and who goes in for Maori women.

Toby Wallop went on, "He has plenty of brown ones up to see him."

"Why not?"

More than likely this scandal has originated in Toby himself. It didn't occur to me to deny it. As it was, Toby himself seemed uneasy, for all his lurid record, in case he was caught drinking alone with me in a deserted whare, and he made a move to go, at which I laughed out loud.

Jonquil said, "Are we going home now, Mummie?"

"Yes. Mr. Toby Wallop is afraid his name might get in the paper."

"No, no," protests. "They'll be waiting on me. They'll be missing the car."

"Oh, he's frightened," I laughed.

Walking together across the wet lush grass to the road he

probed on confidentially, "*Does* old Tom come here to see you?"

"I am married."

"That doesn't mean anything. That's what you told me and Jean six months ago." Bewildered, "That doesn't mean a thing."

"It does with me."

K laughed like anything when he heard and Saul more loudly still.

April 11 · We entertained Saul's brother again at Selah and, selfconscious at this big name in so primitive a place, I fingered my patched green curtains. "When I go to Whanganui if ever I'll buy some new curtains."

"Why have curtains?"

"With flowers on."

"What function have curtains anyway?" Which left me with a recurring question.

Later, when he noticed the words "Nothing matters" printed in charcoal over the fireplace, "Why do you have that there?"

"Because nothing does."

"Some things do." Another haunting question.

And later still, when I had made the tea, although I had not mentioned what I did here, "Isn't it trying having a job and wanting to write? I suppose you don't find much time."

"You have to know how to write."

"Oh, no you don't. But you have to have something to write about."

For the third time I felt a fool that afternoon, though since then I have believed I was right about having to know *how* to write, and that I should have stood my ground. But he, who lived in a posh house in town, was delighted with Selah; I felt the warmth of approval in most of what he said: "How I would like a place like this to do my writing in. Except that when I'm in gear I get dressed up, collar and tie, and even polish my shoes."

"I just undo my brassiere."

That was last week. Today being Saturday, my own Saturday, I came to Selah for a few hours of solid work but I cannot settle. Jonquil wants me to help her build a house for herself, the little boys followed me to the top of the hill and cried when I left, Pauline's stowed-away grief had suddenly surfaced, and K, although he doesn't say so, wants me to talk to while he works outside. I'll remember this day when he's gone, I thought. This will come back and haunt me. So intensely do I feel the need of me at home that for the first time I want to leave Selah. For all I know the Japs might be there. The pull is so burning that I mean to return without even making the tea.

Names of ships like *Neosho*, *Sims* and *Lexington* are handled through the country. True, everyone who shouldn't knows that the American fleet is south of the equator but so is the Japanese fleet. There's a Japanese ship called the *Shosho*, a soft sounding word but with torpedo implications. Where are these two fleets? Carriers, they say.

May · In early May, the beginning of winter, I get back to my books again in the early morning hours after two weeks of preparation for the inspectors. Four-thirty again at last.

For the visit of the inspectors my room was looking just as I had wished. K's was not finished owing to the Home Guard time, but the effect was there. "This," said one, "is what we go about trying to inspire other teachers to do."

"And it's hard," from the senior, "when you can't do it yourself."

"What a beautiful environment for children, Mr. Henderson," from the first. "There's going to be a big fall for these children when you go."

"When you go" is not too good. I'd rather he'd said "If you go."

They discussed the setting with gum Arabic of the Pied Piper on the wall to preserve the impermanent chalk but I didn't take kindly to this idea as the gum would sober the colors. As an alternative, the senior said, "If you care to cut it out this weekend, I'll repaper the wall myself." But I didn't care to cut it down. It belongs up there. Why should it have to last? I like the impermanence of my work on banks and river silt, the most transitory of media . . . the flash of a bird across the water, a passing shower of rain.

It's not good enough to be rushed off to some far-off art gallery where strangers would pay to see it . . . rather friends seeing it without paying. Out of context it would be, whereas here it's a part of our vivid living in the seclusion of the valley, arisen from our living, precipitated by the force of our feeling; even as we have, so has this the right to fade and die.

Although approving of my number scheme which features a mind picture of the panorama of figures, they didn't praise it as Saul's brother did, in spite of their sincere interest. One pointed out the absence of grouping, which I am already thinking out, and the senior was keen to check up on this mind picture several years hence, wondering if it would endure till adulthood, the principle that I claimed.

Their encouragement gave me confidence enough to open up the question that has been engaging me ever since I put my nose into a Maori school—the reading; the absence of any relation between the inside and the outside of a child. I've been sure there was a further step ahead to resolve it and here was my opportunity with inspectors present. After a while I got to the place where I was saying with excitement, "I mean, I . . .

I suppose that schools in the big city slums . . . If I were teaching there I . . . And if I were allowed to I . . . I mean children from criminal homes, starved and that. Throats cut in the night and that sort of thing, hungry, stealing . . . I'd give them words like 'knife' and 'cutthroat' and . . . and 'jail' and 'police' and 'blood.' I'd give them words they lived with."

"Words they lived with," repeated Mr. Harrison.

But he only repeated the last phrase, not stepping forward. It seemed as though he was stalled. "See, what I mean is," I go on, "I'd relate through words the outside of a child to the inside of a child and then you'd get integration."

"And then you'd get integration." No further.

"I've been thinking about this integration business, Mr. Harrison. I think that an integrated person would be a peaceful person. Look how it goes with some people, thoroughly fragmented and not peaceful to know. Disrupting people. I think that an integrated person would end a peaceful person, don't you? A peaceful person?"

"A peaceful person," looking out the door from me to some spot near the pines, as though there were something there, something more important than what I'm saying.

I step nearer to him, hands uplifted. "And a peaceful person, he'd be a worthwhile person. A worthwhile child. Not too naughty."

"Why, are your children naughty, Mrs. Henderson?"

Not the point, damn it. "I suppose they still give them books about the birds in the trees and the breeze and all that, thinking that by giving them peaceful books they'll make the children peaceful. But what they're doing is fragmenting them further, disintegrating them. The thing to do," flash of hands, "is to give them bad books like themselves, then you'd integrate them, then you'd get them peaceful."

"Then you'd get them peaceful," indulgently. "I say, Mr. Henderson," eyes out the door, "where's that spot where you plan to dig a trench for the children? There's no telling when we're going to get this visit from the Pacific. Under the pines over there?"

"Impracticable. You can't dig through the roots. No, Mr. Harrison, I plan it nearer the school, just at the edge of the playground there."

"H'm. Just at the edge of the playground there."

"Lucky, ring the bell please."

The two men spent the weekend with us socially as well as professionally, staying at the House, seeing K's working bee with the school committee on the school wood, going upriver on the boat, attending the school euchre on Saturday night and meeting a gathering of parents, where K introduced them in English and I in Maori. An enlivening breath from the outside world, the professional world, encouraging, and giving us status to ourselves. Plainly we do actually belong to something and are not dispensable units in it. Since then we've treated ourselves with more respect, as being more than pleasant happenings on the River isolated from our kind; being in fact legitimate representatives of a profession, and not such a frightful one either.

· · ·

K is the one to bring news from the village about the far outside world. Last night, "There are four hundred Americans working at Ohakea laying an aerodrome for the Flying Fortresses. They never tell us but evidently the Government is doing something."

"It's unbelievable how used we are becoming to the Japanese invasion. I'm straight-out ashamed."

"I can't see how America can let New Zealand go, the only refueling base for Australia."

It was only yesterday that the submarine shelled California while Mr. Roosevelt was broadcasting.

The Home Guard here has received its orders at last from headquarters at a meeting downriver and a meeting was called of the district to see about carrying them out. There were about forty present, with a good sprinkling of pakehas, with Mr. Snowdon, the big landlord in these parts, in the chair.

There is to be no surrender,
there is to be continued resistance and harassment of the
  enemy,
the Home Guard is to defend its own locality,
the bridges are to be held, blockaded and covered but not
  blown up,
and a trench is to be dug at the school.

Having delivered these orders, Mr. Snowdon discussed a first-aid kit but the subject of laying on water from the river to the pas* where evacuees would be accommodated, and the purchasing of rugs and blankets, brought Harry Rowe to his feet, the two-blooded, barefooted vagabond father of our Holly and Shallcrass, who owned a pa without water and delighted in the distinction of being thought a spy. Who was going to pay for these first-aid kits, rugs and blankets and the laying on of water and who was going to discipline these evacuees from the wicked cities? Until old Matenga, our school-committee chairman, irritably suggested we return to the point and make some effort to stick to it.

Which Mr. Snowdon tried to do, inviting the older Maoris to inspire the younger Maoris at least to join the Home Guard, at which old rich Ponga gave a fiery speech in Maori describing his own prowess with a rifle. Snatching an imaginary rifle, he aimed at us all, then swung into step and marched down the hall, wheeled and marched back again. Rolling his eyes, he mentioned three times the £4,500 he had already given to the war effort, and after another fierce harangue he told us in English, "You don' need some trench. You be alrigh'. I look after you all."

Old Matenga pointed out in angry rapid Maori that trench

* Pa: Maori village.

diggers in the cities were paid; from what source, then, was coming the pay for the Home Guard for digging the school trench? "Me, I old now."

The school trench brought tiny Scotch Mrs. Wallop from the Store to her feet; with trembling voice and a finger to heaven, "You demand to be paid to dig a trench for the children! D'you think the Japs will hold off the invasion until you are paid to dig a trench at the school? You demand payment to defend New Zealand. What sort of country is this? Did our forefathers demand payment to settle here? Yet you are demanding money, money, money to defend it . . . to dig one trench at the school. Money, money, money . . . that's your god!"

She stiffened to her full short stature, which is barely above my shoulders sitting down, her fat white cheeks quivering, the Scotch eyes flinging blue fire, and her forefinger as high as her short arm could reach it. "I myself will organize the women and *we* will dig the trench and *we* won't ask for payment. Shame on you, shame on you, shame on you! I will dig the trench!"

But the Maoris took this benignly enough, being accustomed to Mrs. Wallop behind the counter in the Store.

K rose and pointed out that the question of payment was gathering too much momentum and said, "I know without any doubt that my members of the Home Guard who have stood behind me all this time will be there at six P.M. on Wednesday to dig the children's trench. Nor do I think that the Education Department would mind the school spades being used for that purpose."

The father of our Holly and Shallcrass, Harry Rowe, was the voluntary interpreter between one race and the other throughout, with a relish that was his payment. He lost no opportunities. As the Maori and English speeches followed one another Harry injected more and more of himself into the relaying of them, defending, gratis, his own position on the water at the pa and invariably ending up with an admonition of his own, or an encouragement, wallowing in the last word unconscionably, and having a marvelous time at impersonation: the cold logic of Mr. Snowdon, the irritation of old Matenga, the dramatic illustrations of rich old Ponga—not overlooking the snatching of the imaginary rifle and the marching down the hall, as well as Mrs. Wallop's fiery histrionics complete with pointing finger and quivering cheeks. Oh, we enjoyed Harry Rowe!

Afterwards K and I had a cup of tea with Saul at the cottage, where the three of us talked it over, suddenly believing the war if not the trench. What else could draw such a representative gathering or rouse such feeling?

May 9 · The scare about the Japs so near, up round the Coral Sea area, they say, but there's been a scare of another kind lately—a job in the gazette has attracted K. I never dreamed that it could happen that we'd leave the River, go from the admitted security of it, let alone to a place in the north. For a start K would go into camp, in time leaving me farther from my people than on the Coast, living among strangers and with a much larger school on my hands. And no Saul or anyone like that. Moreover, everyone knows that the enemy will land in the north, could they dodge or defeat the American navy—and teachers up there are already leaving. But when K told me of it over my shoulder when I was playing the march, his excitement firmly registered. "A new open-air school and residence, dear, and a commodious crafts room."

My hands stopped.

"And a full staff."

"But this is where we've felt happy and safe. Where we've spent the happiest year of our lives."

"It's not getting me ahead."

"But it's dangerous up there."

"I'll join the Home Guard."

"But you might go into camp and . . ."

"I haven't gone yet. I can't allow 'mights' to influence me."

Pauline said when we told her, "Don't take any notice of my crying but I can't follow there."

"You might be better at home in Wellington. Bombs or no bombs."

"If only," she cried, "I didn't live between three targets. But the bombers fly very high these days and often miss the target. I might have time to get as far as the nearest evacuation camp, but I'd rather be bombed than that."

"So would I, Pauline. I'd rather catch a bomb in my arms— like this." A cozy nest of my arms.

"So would I!" encircling her arms round an imaginary bomb.

"I'd reach up for it," I said.

"Lord, I do feel better."

Saul wept outright. "I can't bear any more," he said.

· · ·

Two weeks and two days have brought us to winter, yet it's not too cold at Selah. No gale from the south so far has blown the smoke into the room through the cartoon fireplace. Two weeks and three days since I've got to my books, but not because of winter: it's the scare of a "holiday" with K's people looming ahead. How can I do this thing? Serve my family or serve my work? I've got to reconcile the woman and the artist or the conflict between them will blow me asunder, scatter my pieces to the ends of the Pacific . . .

May 22 · Still in the May holidays. Last time I was here at Selah was a fortnight ago, and I ran into an entire hour of cleaning up after the mice. Lunch and a rest before getting to work on the wood with Saul's ax that K has sharpened; furtively wandering about in the winter-wet grass, I collected my indispensable loot.

Fartherest afield first. From the swamp I carried up the mild hill several large armfuls of rotted log, stuff I could dry and use some day when the wind turns round to the south, some evening perhaps when Saul comes to tea. Nearer on the slopes I found odds and bits and I dragged a swag of willow branches from the dell where the water hole is. Nearer still to the whare was overgrown timber and a few abandoned posts, the heavier for back logs against the winter. Those that Mr. Snowdon might question I pulled inside and hid, stacking the porous wet pieces in the fireplace to dry. Then, instead of carrying kindling wood in my haversack from home along with my food and books, I split a supply on the spot. After the idling mind of the "holiday"—the bed-making, talk-making, cake-eating of the last cramped ten days—this was expansion itself, sedation indeed. This gathering of wood in the dignity of the hills . . . restoration indeed.

Yet there is justification of the awful absence, of the torture of halted work. Not that I succeeded in pleasing K or anyone else either—far from it, life forgive me—but it did force results, if unexpected and unforseen by me: from the effort itself to accommodate others and from my hungrier appreciation of Selah I seem to have grown wiser. Moreover, the relief of the silence and loveliness here released a latent idea.

Selah is the house I've built before in the brilliance of wishful fantasy, emerging into reality. This the geography of it. Here could be the fresh air of independence, the miracle of solitude, the pocket of flowers that I saw, of music, study and painting. What I'll do is lease this place from the Native Land Court and fix the whole thing up: the bedroom done in chintz with pretty curtains blowing the dead away, the kitchen equipped as a study and the big front room as a place of music with floor rugs, wine and piano. Elegant people will come with their hair quietly parted. Terrific conversations plunging through till morning, all sorts of heart-to-heart revelations . . . romantic, electric, exclusive. Looking newly at Suicide Cottage I reeled with inspiration.

When the bills are paid and the war is over . . .

·   ·   ·

That was yesterday. Today, my Saturday, I planted sweet peas and nasturtiums that I got through the mail from Yates but in the package I found a letter warning, "You indicated by your order that you were enclosing five shillings but on opening your letter we failed to trace this amount." That money should be owing on joy in the non-money bliss of Selah!

As I sought animal manure and trenched the ground, the necessity to extricate myself from money, live without it possibly, without its values and consequences, pressed on me. The more dearly I loved Selah, the more I was held by the idea of freedom, the independence promising here, the more I vowed to spend no more on my flair for clothes. After all, at least till the war was over, what need had I of clothes? After the war, perhaps a squirrel coat . . .

When I had covered the seeds as firmly as my babies in their cots there was this other matter: the lack of guttering on the roof. Straight from the roof the rain would run carelessly down upon them, gouge them out and wash them away. Along came a stray piece of corrugated iron, which I bent and fixed up there above them, and I cleared the drain that leads to the piping running underground. Finish. No trouble at all.

Of course there were cattle to be kept out of my private back yard somehow; wire, wire netting and such. I pinched each separate finger of hands that belong to a keyboard, but oh, what fun! My idea of a wonderful time. The force of this idea . . .

I was just finishing lunch when Ruth appeared after a morning of work at our place, all glorious black hair and bare feet, to see for herself what was happening up here. In order to utilize the time she was taking I gave her my apple and got her talking. "You knew them, Ruth, Whistle and Mai Mai?"

"A nice apple, Sylv."

"Is it because of the tragedy that the Maoris won't live here?"

"Um. No one live here now. They went away after that and never came back."

"And no other Maoris want to live here either?"

"No."

"Because of that?"

"Yes."

A step nearer to my possession of Selah. "Mr. Snowdon," I said, "he only leases the property. Who are the real owners, Ruth?"

"Oh, a lot of them."

"Is it under the Native Land Court?"

"Um, that's it."

"Why didn't the Old One let Whistle marry Mai Mai?"

"Too young, I suppose. A schoolgirl. You should have a nice piece of iron on that hearth, Sylv."

"I'll have it bricked, Ruth, in time, when the war is over. Too young? I heard it was because the Old One wanted Mai Mai to marry a white man with money who was living with them."

"Perhaps. Oh, Mai Mai was a lovely girl, Sylv."

"Yes, I could tell by the books she left at school. Tidy writing."

"Oh, she could sing too, Mai Mai."

"So they say. Tell me, who was living here at the time it happened?"

"Laa. Working down at the House there. And her mother."

"Mrs. Hohepa?"

"That's right. Mrs. Hohepa and Laa."

"And don't they want to come back and live here?"

"No, no. They won't come back. They've never once been back since that day."

"Ruth . . . where were Mrs. Hohepa and Laa when it happened?"

"They were down at the pa with their people. New Year's Eve." So reluctant is Ruth that I should stop this probing, but I can't.

"And where was Whistle living?"

Ruth munched unhappily at her apple. "He was living here too."

"With the two Hohepas?"

"Um."

"Was he here on New Year's Eve?"

"No. He was down at the pa with the others. All at the pa."

"And when did he and Mai Mai come up here together?"

"That night."

"New Year's Eve?" I had to check constantly on her vagueness.

"Yes. He brought the girl up here on New Year's Eve."

Stop. But I didn't. "And when did Mrs. Hohepa find them?"

"She came back the next day to get some clothes."

"I heard she saw them through the window."

"No. She came right inside and looked in there—" she nodded her head toward the doom room—"and saw them. She locked the door and went away and told the others."

"And she never came back again?"

"Never came back again. Never any more."

"And who came and got the bodies?"

"The policeman and the detective."

I asked, "And is this whare tapu now?"

Ruth laughed nervously but didn't reply. We both looked into the flames and she said, "You want to fix your chimney,

Sylv, and put a bricks in here. Make it smaller."

"I want it big like that, Ruth. I wonder why they did it."

"A love," wistfully. "Tha's a good kettle, Sylv."

"My mother gave it to me. Where were they buried?"

"Oh, Mai Mai was buried in the Old One's graveyard—you know, by Mrs. Hira's place? And Whistle . . . he was buried in the Hohepa graveyard way downriver. The Old One she said, 'They lie together in life but they won't lie together in death.' "

"A love," I said.

"A love, Sylv."

Soon after that Ruth showed me where the daffodils were under the ground outside and she sang going back down the road, her voice reaching over the valley and swamp where the water hole is—bell-like. As though she were singing close at hand, as though Mai Mai were singing close at hand. Re-entering the whare slowly I felt their presences all over again in the doll-like bedroom there; felt them for the first time since the children dispersed them months ago now, when K and Pauline were here.

A love, I thought, and turned to my books. A love, I thought, as I walked down the road in the enchanted twilight —a love and Saul.

At home I gauged the overall, all-round climate on both sides of the road to be sufficiently permissive for me to spend an evening of music with Saul, and I dressed before the evening meal in Pauline's pink frilled organdie blouse, at which she looked at me covertly across the table. "I always thought, you know, that youth was the time for beauty. I was a fool. I can look far better now than I used to. As for you . . ." Overtly now she gazed at my hair and the geranium in it. "What a lovely color that flower is. My word, I do think your hair suits you long like that. My word, you do look something."

None of which was as convincing as K's remark when he called at the cottage later with Saul's medical mail—no, the next morning he said it. "You always do look pretty, dear, but really . . . last night!"

May 24 · My own legitimate Sunday the following day. I've had a wonderful day's work with no interruptions, not even anxiety about the Pacific or whether Saul loves me. No one has said anything, of course, about the South Pacific but there's a general feeling that the Japs might not be coming, not in the immediate future. Not that we know what's happened but somebody did say there has been a frightful battle in the Coral Sea area and that the United States lost it, as well as the *Lexington*, the *Sims* and the American *Neosho;* that they were torpedo-bombed—but that the encounter was sufficient to trip up the Japs on their way to us. We don't actually *know*. But the general relaxation in the country has reached even to us in our upriver retreat and I've had a good day's work.

There was first, however, a short delay while I admired the success of my plumbing; while the rain obliged, as it has for a year, I watched my guttering in action, enthralled. *Marvelous* where joy can burst from, cascading like the water. And it's marvelous where rain can come from, cascading like the joy. It poured all day as I sat at my books, when I stoked the fire with my happy wood, happily gathered wood, my well-gotten loot, and while I lunched. Oh, what rapture can come one's way in the wreck of a haunted whare!

· · ·

At four I changed into the scarlet blouse that Saul likes so much and at half past four he arrived as arranged, looking wonderfully handsome with his black hair brushed and the smartest new tie, for a cup of tea and a talk—talk which fused with the slipping dusk and sloping candlelight and with the spirit of the whare itself . . . timelessly. Into the evening conversation flowed amid the listening ghosts when mortals

should not be here. Indeed in the denial of physical love . . .
passion vaporized . . . two mortals were not here. But in case
K should be waiting for me—and it turned out that he was—
we came to a close at midnight. I spent an hour in his bed
recounting this conversation. My blessed safety valve.

·   ·   ·

Ravishing the days since I came home. But school reopens
on Monday, when I revert to the after-school dashaway, leaving the children to Pauline. Not that I'll be able to get my
daily ration of silence with the winter days shortening. To
hook off home before dark I have to stop at a quarter to five,
no more than an hour and a half-odd. I'll have to think of
something else. At least I bag two hours in the early morning
at home, which I've begun again.

Saul said he knew for a fact that the Japanese carrier *Shosho*
had been sunk up in the Coral Sea, and a few smaller vessels,
and that the battle, while a strategic win for the States, was
a tactical win for the Japs—whatever that might mean. But we
still don't know whether they're coming or not. In the meantime the school children find any number of other uses for the
trench.

May 29 · When I got to school, I ran away again in despera-
tion for my ration of solitude, without which I cannot operate
as a teacher, mother, wife or lover. I'm nullified without it.
Like water from a creek to a vagabond, it is necessary to me.
All right—I'm not at school this afternoon, but I'd never be
there at all without this wetting of my mouth in the waters of
silence. We all have the right to self-preservation, personally
as well as nationally. But at Selah the wind is from the south
and I run into the thickest fire-smoke from the defective chimney and the thickest of winter drafts, so that I wish I had
stayed at school.

June 6 · That wonderful return to Selah, like that wonderful battle of Midway, is now two weeks of school behind, two weeks without a Saturday. At last I got here late this morning. A rare and beautiful day it is, stealthily escaped from the rain, more so at Selah. Blue milk and yellow honey. For a while before I began on the wood, when I sat on the rugged step, I became the day itself.

Having already raided the nearer sources I had to loot farther afield. From the closer slopes I pulled manuka brush, chopped it with Saul's ax and stacked it on the porch. Then there was this matter of the path in the yard from the gate to the steps, which in the winter rains needed a touch of gravel. Gravel . . . let me see . . . gravel. There was gravel on the road out there, there was my haversack and billy, the head of a spade without a handle, and finally there was I. No reason for no gravel on my path except for the guilt of pilfering. But who would miss a few handfuls of gravel from a lonely highway? Yet the guilt made it hard—the actual furtive scooping it up, looking this way and that between puffing . . . the reaching hands, the filling of the haversack and billy.

When it came to the lifting of them I had the greatest difficulty getting the haversack up on my back—too, too heavy. Finally I pulled myself erect by the fence but oh, life! Oh, the joy of spreading this gravel on the one-man path—seeing in mind the elegant feet that would tread this path as well as my family's and Saul's, and indeed my own, during future winters. The whole thing called for celebration, which took the form of eating apples, sitting and gazing incredulously at the dream-coming-true before me.

After which I papered the walls till five, finishing the lot. To describe this day as ecstatic will have to do, for where is the word that includes in its syllables the healing in these hours, the mending of dessicated nerve-ends and the water it gave to the spirit—that incorporates the feel of the gravel in my furtive palms, the sound of the manuka dragging behind over forgiving grass? Can you put mad heaven into a word or must it remain unwritten?

K has to go to the war euchre tonight so I'll hurry home now. No time to call in at Saul's.

June 7 · Today, Sunday, K gave me also. Some wives ask their husbands for clothes, for money, houses or glamorous trips, but all I ask is "a day." And what did he do? He gave me two. Far more than a husband to me, a built-in lover and a father to the children, he is the mother of us all. True, I did leave Ruth nominally in charge at home, if her slow long-haired smiling nonaction can be termed "in charge," but I know where the children will be.

But one cannot recapture, repeat the realms of yesterday. Actually I should have been writing—so much omitted from this record such as K's improvements here, the little gate he made to the yard and an extraordinary conversation with Saul about old age, perspective, design, what-about-life and featuring a wheelchair metaphor . . . but during the morning I white-calcimined the walls and scrubbed the floor afterward and in the afternoon instead of sitting at my table I lay on the bed with the master of all headaches. Until Saul came to afternoon tea, but I hurried home to the children and my best friend—codeine—and to get ready for the War Institute in the evening. How I hate being president! How I resent the time from my work, attending these piffling functions!

. . .

"There's just one *question*," from Mrs. Blom, who lives in isolation across the river, "I would like to ask Mrs. K. Where is the parcel—" a dull nagging voice—"the war parcel that was arranged to be sent for the second time?"

"Oh yes, that . . ."

"It was donated and arranged to be sent," she said.

"Oh *yes*—I remember."

"Yes, Mrs. K, you had it all down."

"I did. So I did. It's just here somewhere." I began turning over the multitudinous papers, adding with less certainty, "Just here somewhere . . ."

Mrs. Blom pursued sepulchrally, "You had them all down."

By this time I could see it was not "just here" and, closing the folder, "Oh, we had a very very long meeting last time. I think we'll have a nice short one this time." Glancing at Mrs. Blom with apprehension, I found her shaking with laughter.

. . .

Yet I do write a little today. Still stinging from the behavior of the children that Monday when I ran away from school, I put down the outlines of a story I'll tell them one of these days. They're always so good after a story if it's a well-chosen one, and by well-chosen I don't mean some traditional one from the imposed culture like Red Riding Hood or Jack and the Beanstalk, but one about themselves, relating the outside to the inside. They are good for weeks then, as though I'd given them a dose of sedative. That Monday I ran away . . . their atrocious behavior and my atrocious behavior . . . the stinging humiliation of it.

I'll tell them this story tomorrow:

. . .

Once upon a time there was a school on a hill full of very naughty children. Know what they used to do? They'd quarrel with each other, tread on their books, leave their dusters all over the floor and chuck their chalk in the fireplace. When the teacher turned her back to write on the blackboard they'd stop their work and get up to all sorts of mischief, and if she had to leave the room for anything,—if one of her little boys was crying—they'd throw the clay about, or rather the boys did. But worst of all, the most bad-mannered of all, when she was teaching, they'd talk at the same time and didn't know what she was saying.

One afternoon when they were worse then usual the teacher said to them, "I've had enough of this school. You are all far too naughty, except Tiny. I'm going away and I'll never come back." And that's exactly what she did. She walked out the door, down the steps and didn't come back.

For a while they had a lovely time without any teacher. They stopped their work, threw their books on the floor and walked over them, talked out loud, stood on desks, threw clay about, which stuck to the walls too high up to reach, made each other cry with teasing and hitting until finally, not being able to be any naughtier, they went out and ran off home.

They stayed at home for weeks. They swam in the river, climbed the trees, looked for birds' nests and played by the lake in the hills. "Gee, how corker without any school!" you would hear them saying. "We'll never go back."

In time, however, Tiny was worried to be missing all those lessons and she said to Pearly, "I've had enough of no school. I think I'll go back and try to remember how to read and write. The white children of the guests at the House can read and everyone knows how to write, but I've forgotten how to. I wonder if my books are still there."

" 'Course they're there," said Pearly. "Your books are on the floor by the hearth. I threw them there myself."

"Well, you shouldn't have, Pearly," Tiny said. "I want to use them again."

That very morning Tiny washed her face and hands, combed her long hair and walked up the hill to the school. It was not pleasant when she got there because there was no sound of voices. No one was playing on the grass or hiding in the trench and nobody rang the bell. Worst of all, there was no teacher there to say, "Good morning, Tiny." No one cared about her.

In time she walked up the steps and across the porch and into the children's room. The doors were still open, as the children had left them, banged about by the wind; so were the windows open, and the birds had been in—you could see their droppings on the floor and splashed upon the desks. And rats had chewed the edges of the new books in the cupboard and there were spiders in the rafters. It was a doleful sight. Tiny stood within the door and shed two sad tears. How terrible it looks, she thought, not like our school at all.

Just at that moment she heard a voice, and whom did she see but a round-eyed owl on a back desk, and do you know what he was doing? He was holding a pencil in his claw and was trying to do his writing. "Good morning, Tiny," said the owl. "And how are you today?"

"Good gracious," she said. "What are you doing here?"

"I'm doing my work, of course."

"But this is not your school," she said. "This is our school."

"It is my school now," said Olliphant Owl. "You children don't seem to want it. Here I am and here I stay." And he went on with his writing.

"What are you writing, Olliphant Owl? There's nothing on the blackboard."

"I'm making it up," said the owl. "I'm writing about this school. About the chalk in the fireplace and the books on the floor and the clay stuck on the walls. When I've finished I'll take it home to the forest and read it to the birds."

"No, don't do that," Tiny said. "The teacher wouldn't like it. She tried to make it a lovely school; it's we children who have spoiled it."

"The teacher?" said Olliphant. "I see no teacher."

"No, she's gone away."

"Where?" asked Olliphant Owl.

"I've no idea," said Tiny and shed three more tears.

"That's bad luck," said the owl. "I could honestly do with a teacher. There's a whole lot of words I want to use but I don't know how to spell them. How do you spell 'Andrew'?"

"I don't know," she said. "I used to know but I've forgotten now." Another tear fell. "Why what are you writing about Andrew?"

"About how he was pushing Eva's arm when Eva was doing her drawing. Can you spell 'Pearly' then?"

"No, I've forgotten that too. What are you writing about Pearly?"

"About when she cries for nothing. How she yells at the top of her voice for nothing and we hear her in the forest. Can't you remember how to spell any names at all?" The owl looked disappointed.

"All I can remember how to spell is my own name, Tiny. T-i-n-y," she spelled.

"But I knew that one," he said. "It was a such a little one. I've finished writing about you."

"What did you write about me?" she asked, stepping a little nearer.

"I wrote good things about you. About how you liked working and never talked or threw clay on the walls, and how clever you were at spelling. But I'll have to cross that out. You can't spell now at all."

"Yes I can, yes I can!" And Tiny ran to the fireplace, and there she picked up some yellow chalk and wrote her name on the blackboard. Then she picked up Jacob's book from the floor and copied his name on the blackboard. She looked for other books about the room, half-eaten by the rats, and wrote the names on the board. "See?" she said. "I can so spell."

"You're not a bad little teacher," said the owl. "I've been very short of a teacher. Will you hear me my spelling, Tiny?"

"But that's Bernard's book you're using," she said.

"Of course it is Bernard's book. There's hardly anything in

it, that's why. He must have been a lazy boy."

For the rest of the day Tiny was the teacher and taught Olly a lot of words, and on the way home in the afternoon when she met her friend, Eva, she told her all about it.

"I'll come tomorrow," Eva said. "I've forgotten my spelling too."

So the next day there were three at school: Tiny, Eva and Olliphant the Owl. Eva washed the birds' droppings off her desk and cleaned out the rat's nest inside it and, after a lengthy search, picked her book from inside the piano where Olga had hidden it and found a pencil outside on the grass, then settled down to work. And there they were with Tiny the teacher all day long till evening.

On her way home Eva told Airini, who said she'd come to-morrow, and this went on day after day as more children returned to school, so that in time the whole lot were back. And there was no more of this talking and jumping and yelling and throwing things about, but a good deal of very nice work. "You crowd are not as bad as I thought," said Olliphant the Owl. "Not like you used to be. If you'd been good like this before, your teacher would never have left. And I bet if she knew you were like this now she'd think about coming back. Does anyone know where she is?"

"No," said the children, "we've no idea. Not one of us has seen her since."

"When I go home tonight," said the owl, "I'll tell the other birds about it and ask them to look for her, if you like. They know the hiding places."

"But before you do that," Tiny said, "we'll have to clean the room. She hated it being dirty. She couldn't stand the dusters on the floor and the chalk under foot, and when we trod on the books. Tomorrow we'll spend the day cleaning up the room and putting the things away, and getting the clay marks off the walls, and washing out after the rats."

"I'll do the cupboard," said Eva.

"I'll do the table," said Pearly.

"We'll do the floor," said Airini and Lovey, and Huhua and Arihi.

"And we'll get the clay marks off the walls," said Jacob and Rikirangi.

"And I'll clean the blackboards," said Horowhenua, and, "I'll find the chalk," said Ru.

At the end of the next day the schoolroom was lovely, just as the teacher liked it. "All we've got to do now," said Olliphant the Owl, "is to somehow bring back the teacher. The moment I get home I'll put the birds on the job who know all her hiding places."

June 14 · I'm at Selah; it's Sunday again. After getting well up the road before remembering my keys, I didn't get here till ten-thirty. Then there was the fire to light, water to bring, cups to wash after the sudden flight home before dark last Sunday, the place to tidy up, the sweet-pea seedlings to be admired, lunch to have and myself to orient for Saul—to somehow lever myself from this other world into that of edged reality, to talk, if possible, rationally. All of which took till one P.M.

But I'm weary for work today. After the euchre aggregate last night there followed at Saul's place four hours of solid row until three A.M. He wanted to unburden many controversial things fermenting in his mind, in the interests of peace between us. He wanted to know if he had hurt me, how he had hurt me and if I would tell him. He asked me if I still loved him and, above all, should K go into camp, if I could live with him, to all of which I had to confess that although I could never never live with him, I could not, in fact, live without him near.

"I thought," he said, "you didn't love me, because you said you couldn't live with me."

"That doesn't mean I don't love you. I just do, that's all, whether I can live with you or not."

"I'm in that kind of doubt all the time. For a while I think you do, then a look, or something you say, makes me . . . and then . . . I know I've hurt you."

"I repeat, I love you. I'm saying it. The hurts are due to my affliction of oversensitivity, or sheer irritability, to be frank, rather than to any roughness from you. They are not your responsibility. And they don't matter, even if they were." Anything but the "utter truth." "I just put them aside and they fade away from simple lack of attention." Lies.

"I wish you would tell me what the hurts are. It'll help me not to hurt others. I would be very grateful."

"Well, I won't. I'll leave any further criticism of you to some worthier person who has the intellectual and moral qualifications for analyzing others. I need to be a reasonably worthy person myself first, which I'm not. Besides . . . I did do that once, and look at the chaos! I love you. Did I forsake you for the length of a minute over that ravishing young inspector? Haven't I been faithful to you all this time?"

Faint surprise, "Yes."

"I love you but I can't live with you. In the first place you could never stand up to my vagaries and in the second place I could never stand up to the repercussions they bring on me from you. In any case, owing to my chronic irritability, I couldn't live with anyone at all."

"You manage to live with Keith."

"Oh . . . well . . . that's different."

"A mere vagary, I presume."

I was terribly aware that my work would pay, how my one weekly day's precious work would fail after such late hours, but I couldn't bring myself to stop. I could not break off in the middle of the intricate nocturnal hair-splitting, having no taste for unfinished things. Cheerfully I surrendered the night

hours, uncharacteristically—most uncharacteristically—taking
the blame for the pain between us but with only a fifty per
cent chance of convincing him. So my work failed today, my
once-a-week quotient. Damn!

Then Saul came as arranged this afternoon, an experiment
of mine to see if I could work in his presence, in which case I
could kill two birds with one stone—conduct two loves with
one stone, at one time, Saul and work, which I know in ad-
vance I can not. Although some of the spadework should be
possible—word study, quotations and such—or would be,
were he not at this moment eating his lunch sitting on the bed,
never knowing the torture of that crunching. O dolorous fall
from paradise! Where is that rapture of a week ago gathering
wood and gravel? True, Saul has brought some work to do,
his TB charts, in This Awful Place, but as I told the mason bee
months ago there's room for only one in Selah.

· · ·

One day in the June of winter, I had not been home from
the Store ten minutes when K said over the table, "Did you
know about the ballot?"

A parcel I was putting down paused in mid-air, and I
studied his face.

Evenly, "It's from thirty-two, thirty-three . . ."

He'd missed it.

". . . thirty-four."

"Have you seen your name in it?"

"The gazette won't be out till the twenty-third. This was
only in the paper."

"I'll have to learn to milk Susie."

· · ·

On June 23 K was called up, his notice in the mail, so we
didn't apply for the school up north and I faced the prospect
of Susie. The thing about milking Susie is that K doesn't bail

her up, thinking it might hurt her feelings, he being too fond
of her to submit her to such gross indignity, but he milks her
as she stands in the middle of the paddock. A fiery young Jersey with ideas of her own, but she responds adoringly to K, as
he strokes her under the chin and calls her "darling." "Little
darling," you hear him.

After she had kicked my bucket over three times and hurled
me prostrate I said, "Why don't you bail her up?"

"She doesn't need bailing up. It's a matter of understanding
her. Learning how to handle her."

"All other cows get bailed up. It's uncivilized not to bail her
up. Why shouldn't she be bailed up too? What's she got that
other cows haven't?"

"Personality. I'm used to the character of a fiery young Jersey. I've lived ten years with one. Anyway I've got no bail and
there isn't the need for one. Fiery women are better without
hindrance."

"If you don't build a bail, you can't go to war."

Rather huffily K milked her himself again, stroking her chin
and crooning, "Never mind, little darling."

"Funny how you stroke her under the chin and call her
little darling. Why don't you do it to me?"

"She's calm again now, look. Try again. Now don't upset
her. Win her confidence."

"To hell with her confidence! I'm not stroking and little-
darling her. You attend to that end and I'll attend to this."
The bucket in one corner, I in another, and Susie in the heart
of the forest.

·   ·   ·

On Saturday night a notice from the Education Department lodging an appeal with the Public Service Commission
against the calling up of any more teachers, so we could have
applied for the school up north and I could have ceased my
acquaintance with Susie—much to the relief of Susie. But

when K passed his medical frightfully A 1 I didn't know what to do about her though she knows what to do about me.

July 19 · Into July now. July the night of winter, and five weeks since I've been here at Selah. One Saturday K was ill, I remember, and another the children were, all from this flu he brought from town when he went for his medical. Another Saturday the day was ill—a herculean storm of rain and cold and I knew smoke would hurl round the room, as on that Monday escaped from school, so although K was helping me to get away I decided to work in the school instead, the tall secure school where he had prepared a fire of hissing manuka, where there were no drafts, no smoke, no meals to prepare, and where there was plenty of room to spread open my big chart of the centuries. Another Saturday I was ill, not from the popular flu but a herculean storm of tears at having to leave the children so I couldn't come. Which leaves one Saturday unaccounted for. What was the reason that day in the language of herculean storms—Home Guard for K or Saul Guard for me?

Although I have been longing to see the seedlings, the gravel on the path, and whether the grass in the yard is greener, I knew I couldn't stick it. I couldn't work in the cold and smoke of nature, the smoke and cold of the heart, but after the convulsions yesterday of both the weather and me, this Sunday opened like a water lily and K said to me, "I want you to have this day."

He got me off quite early, and as I picked my way up the scoured road still running with rills from yesterday's storm, pausing at the overfull waterfalls, as I padded barefoot beneath dripping trees to the baa of the sheep echoing in the hills and the cheeky chat of the magpies, it occurred to me that it could be the topography of the valley itself, as violent as it is beautiful, that engendered the drama in our lives, and that if ever we found ourselves living on some stark plain we would settle for calmer patterns. O blessed thought!

I found a beast had been in my yard, a sheep, by the droppings. Not much damage but the path was spoiled.

I brought my paints and chalk today, and after painting a square of wall with blackboard paint I drew an exciting lady —sophisticated. And I painted a watercolor of Beethoven for Saul, to smooth over the "swift mistaken word; the unmeant wrong." We tried valiantly at the time to ignore it; apparently I had implied that he interrupted my work. "Oh," he said, "I thought I'd write for an application form for the medical unit."

I looked at him sitting desolate in his bed, wan and wrought. "And you've had only one day of misery and not even a night."

"Yes . . . one evening."

He'd wept all night then. "And did you expect me to come tonight?"

"I don't know." His silly pajamas . . .

"You did expect me. You knew very well I'd come."

"Well, I thought you might."

"And what if I myself enlisted in the Waafs or the Wrens or the Waacs or something, and you'd never see me again?"

"Last evening I couldn't picture me without you."

"It happens to a lot of people, you know."

"Darling, I do love you."

I sipped my wine.

"Do you think I haven't had enough pain?" he asked.

"Not by a long way. But I'll leave it to someone else to give it to you. *I* won't any more, in fact I can't."

"Darling, I do love you."

I sipped my wine—again.

"What shall I do about myself?"

"Trust me."

"I do."

"No. You suspect just about everything I say."

"What are you thinking?" forever watching my face.

"I'm just trying to pull myself together to go home."

I put down my glass and he held both my hands. "What are you thinking?" he asked again.

"That I love you very much" . . . valiantly, but it blew up regardless, like the last time.

Inadvertently this second portrait of Beethoven was better than the first that I did, a wedding anniversary present for K next month, and for a time I thought I would switch them, but as every line of the second was done for Saul I'd give it to him when he came to meet me at five.

Also during the day I was reading about Rembrandt and found between him and Beethoven a remarkable likeness, in their craving for liberty and their impatience with the orthodox. Ah . . . I understand them!

I've had a wonderful day, not only because of the silence, or because the fire worked with no smoke blowing, or because I was working with color, but because of the harmony between me and K—for the time being. Between K and my work I mean, as miraculous as harmony between husband and lover. To realize this as we did yesterday is to take hold of stars in your hands. In and out of the storms we've been much in love. I think he is always, but he reveals it in ratio to the opportunity my variable behavior allows. I've been grateful for this blessed state of affairs, not least on account of the independence of others it gives me. What of love and understanding an artist seeks I often find at home.

July 21 · When K returned from Home Guard last night to find me crying and asked me what for, I replied, "I've failed you so badly."

"I consider you one of the few successes of my life."

The evening resolved itself into one of reconciliation and

intense love; for hours we knew that oneness. "I love you," I told him. "I love you more than anyone in the world."

"I need your love," he said. "When I know you love me I feel I can achieve anything."

At the end of the evening he sent me across the road to Saul for a change of air. Saul put his hands on my shoulders. "You are a habit with me," he said, "just like food and clothes. And just as necessary."

> If it were now to die
> 'Twere now would be most happy, for I fear
> My soul hath her content so absolute
> That not another comfort like to this
> Succeeds in unknown fate.

·IV·

July 23 · The other day after school Saul brought Dr. Blakely into Selah, another TB man, a reserve occupation, soon after I'd settled down, and to utilize the time with them I steered the conversation to the tragedy room again. I gave them tea by the fire, then opened, "It was at the New Year I believe."

Saul said, "Yes."

"Doctor said, "Yes, I remember. New Year's Day. I remember I had something all planned for that day. I *was* annoyed."

"Did you come out here, Doctor?"

"I did, and when I was away two babies I was booked for were born. Nurse attended them. When I got home she said, 'I've had a couple of babies,' and I said, 'I've sewn up a couple of throats.'"

"Did you have to sew them, Doctor?"

Saul asked, "Wasn't one cut from ear to ear?"

"The girl it was," said Doctor. "The head was right back and you could see the spinal column."

I hadn't pictured that in the other room.

"And," he went on, "the boy just a slit at the wrist and another at the throat."

"Just little ones on the boy!"

"Oh, yes. He made sure of Mai Mai but he couldn't have

succeeded with himself, with the radial artery, so had to do his throat. Both small wounds."

He stretched a foot to the flame. "In a double tragedy like that the first act is done in a moment of madness and the second in panic."

"It must have been nearly cut off," from Saul.

"It actually was."

Saul had to walk all the way home with me that night, through the school gate, up the hill and to our very door.

July 24 · Still July in winter. When I went to school this morning I had a surprise for I found all my little sick ones back after their colds, and where I had had seven or eight of them last week I had twenty-eight today including two brand-new ones: an infinitesimal boy and, believe it or not, blind Kata Ponga.

I expected her to be extra shy but as I watched her standing in the doorway between Olga and Rosie Tahore I had a feeling that she wasn't and that her stillness had its source in alert attention. Moreover, her uplifted face was serene, a lilt at the corners of her mouth and her big eyes glancing upward from side to side make me think she was watching something glorious flying to and fro.

I told Olga to sit her on a small chair by the fire, from habit thinking that a small new one would be nervous at a desk, and I put Jonquil's doll in her arms. Then, forgetting the urgency of my preparation for such unexpected numbers and oblivious of the liquid sound of running voices in the room, I stood a moment and watched her.

At once she began excitedly to mother the doll, her hands almost quivering with sensitivity as she felt over it feverishly and lovingly. She stroked and patted it as her own mother must have done, yet much more passionately, a mothering more intense than anything I had seen in a child; her hands seemed to speak.

As for shyness she seemed to have none at all, perhaps because she couldn't see the strangeness of us, yet for a while before I'd given her the doll she had certainly felt us. I didn't mistake that absolute stillness of receptivity at the door—and she still did feel us, though she didn't speak as she warded off the heat from the blazing manuka on her bare legs, and when I asked Olga to move her further from it she still didn't say anything although I felt the inner alertness. Then I had to get on with my preparation for the other twenty-seven.

Later on I remembered to tell Olga, who was the doll monitor, to get the doll's bed, but Kata didn't know what it was and it was I who put it on her knee and said, "This is a bed for the doll, Kata."

At once the sensitive hands started on it, balancing the stuffing of the mattress and smoothing it better than I could myself with two good eyes to aid me.

Soon she was talking and laughing to herself as I've seen her do down in the pa, and when Ru with his hooligan blood sniggered and drew attention to it I spoke to him sharply. Not that Kata would have known had they laughed at her.

When I let them all out at playtime I had to tell Kata, but she said, her eyes flinging to and fro as though following flying things above, "I take the doll, Mrs. Henderson."

"No, you can't take the doll, Kata. Not outside." I knew how long the doll would last once the small boys got hold of it. Besides, toys have this way of disappearing, once through the schoolroom door, and I mean to preserve my collection. Also this doll was the prewar doll with sleeping eyes off the market for years that I'd brought home to Jonquil on the Coast after being away from her so long.

Kata said instantly, "I stay by the doll."

"No. You go outside now, Kata, for some sun and cocoa.

Leave the doll here and when you come back you can have it again."

Olga took her out, although she didn't appear to need much taking; it seemed she could see by the confident way she made for the door and the steep steps beyond . . . this trust she had in the world about her.

In no time she was back. On her own, feeling her way eagerly through the door, her face uplifted, her eyes flashing upward. "I come back to the doll."

So I gave her the doll. "Take the doll outside, Kata, and bring it back when you come in again." How did she come to be so obedient? No bullying in her background—her father and mother were the most easy-going of Maoris.

During the second half of the morning she became hilarious with herself with a stream of laughter and chatter. She put the doll to bed, she took it out. She hitched it on her back Maori-fashion. She took off its bonnet and put it on herself. She tucked the doll in again, arranged its pillows, sang to it, rocked the bed like a pram, and all the time these hands patted feverishly and sensitively, her face turned upward, her eyes on something wonderful above. Many times during the noisy business of teaching I paused to watch her, and to say once or twice, "Softer, Kata. I can't hear the other children," at which the crowing voice lowered.

By this time I thought she could stand the strangeness of a desk, and at my touch she responded instantly and felt round the corners of the desk, and when I pressed her shoulders and said, "Sit down, Kata," you'd think she'd always known there was a seat there and that she had often sat on it. Her trust did hurt.

But when lunchtime came and Olga, whose responsibility the doll was, snatched it to put it away, "That's mine!" from Kata. The eyes still chasing the darting things above, she unable to pursue the thief.

"Give it back, Olga. She doesn't know you are only putting it away." And when Olga did I said, "We are just putting the doll away for lunchtime, Kata. When you come back you can have it again."

"I take the doll home, Mrs. Henderson."

"No, you can't take the doll home, Kata. You can have it again when you come back from lunch."

At once she gave up the doll to Olga. "I come back to the doll."

But she didn't. In the afternoon the rest of us were bowled over by a flying theme: strange, brilliantly colored flying things the children were drawing—darting birds, dragonflies, flitting fairies, cruising angels, shooting stars in abandoned gorgeous designs . . .

August 1 · For exactly twelve days it has been too cold to come to Selah and in fact still is. Will the day ever come in the long life ahead when I'll have a warm place to work, as warm as the schoolroom when I use it, but without its overtones, when I don't have to leave my cozy home and face a bitter morning? A place of beauty, silence and comfort with no drafts, no smoke and no distance from home? I assured myself it would.

But although I carried these warm hopes within me and although I had left home the earliest yet, nine A.M., a bleak mist met me as well as a frost, and the walk was the least pleasant yet—spitefully bitter to me like the tongue of Saul turned sourly against me: "How I hate you," I said, "for the way you can throw me out of your mind the moment I've gone. Just toss your head and reach for the paper."

He laughed delightedly.

I said, "Oh, I know how to cure that, of course . . . if I were not so soft."

"You might kill something."

"Oh no, I won't."

"You would kill something."

"Oh no, I wouldn't. I know. I know that I couldn't."

"Now don't . . . don't . . ." hesitated.

"Show off?" I supplied.

"Yes."

"Do you think I'm showing off?"

"Yes."

"I'm not showing off."

He watched me in silence.

"You coax and cajole me to say these things and when I do you say I'm showing off."

"I didn't ask you to prescribe a cure."

The jagged edge to his tongue. He watched on, watched me.

"I hope," I said "you will accept my deepest apology for such presumption."

He laughed again. "Oh no, I'm enjoying it!"

It was time for me to run.

. . .

Walking up the road in the bitter morning I wasn't very happy. I was crying, in fact, at the latest triangular upheaval brought on by my passions. "I want to know," I told K when he returned from the milking, "if you are satisfied with me as a wife and a mother."

He strained the milk and didn't answer.

"You must allow," I defended, "for the six hours at school taken from my day that another wife would use for mending and that, and thinking of things for you and the little ones."

Reservedly, the strainer pausing, "Yes I'm satisfied," but it didn't sound like it.

Would the day ever come in the life ahead when I would be innocent of passion or could at least relate passion to reason? That was something of which I could not assure myself. As I plodded round the corners in coat, gum boots and K's big gloves, haversack weighted on back, I could not see myself at all becoming a "worthwhile person."

I climbed the road gate, walked across the grass, and as I approached the whare after a fortnight's absence I said to myself aloud, "I wonder what blow awaits me here."

I could see no animal had been in but the wind had blown down the manuka standing against the fence and I picked it up with gloved hands, going over the whole yard retrieving other bits, and I found that the magpies had pulled some nasturtium, a worse blow than I was braced for, which I replaced glove-handed. After which, since there were no other blows, I got to work on the fire and brought the water.

Having used the last of the tank-stand posts, I had no back-log, so I wandered after something else, but although I couldn't find anything I still resisted Mr. Snowdon's fence posts and fell back on my store of manuka. It was about ten A.M. before I took off my things and settled down to work on the low iron stool, thawing my toes and reading Russell's *Power*. Then pulled the chair over for a table and did my real writing—my novel called *Rangatira*.

Toward noon a Maori parent came in, Mrs. Ponga, blind Kata's mother all eyes and curiosity, at which I took off time for lunch. Little did she know her value to me as she enlarged on the story of the lovers. Characteristically the whole point of their story has been the last to come out . . . the reason *why* they did it. She told me that Whistle was due to be arrested that very New Year's Day for having a girl under age.

"This place is haunted," she said. "I wouldn't live here for quids."

I didn't intend anyone to want to live here for quids. "You're dead right," I said, "it is. I wouldn't sleep here at night."

Easily, so easily, the gentle casual visitor continued supplying the artist with raw material. She told me she kept little blind Kata home from school because Rosie and Olga and them had left her behind on their way back from lunch in the village to school, that the pig had chased her and that in panic and blindness she had run straight into the creek: "Mud! Mud on her face, mud on her clothes, mud on her hands and legs . . . all cover' in mud."

When Mrs. Ponga had gone I spent much of the afternoon writing these two stories, utterly forgetting the bitterness of the morning—about my small blind pupil at school and about Whistle and Mai Mai. Toward evening when I'd finished, however, on my way home I didn't call in at Saul's or go up to our house, but called into the schoolroom and got the doll and ran down the road with it to the pa where Kata was sitting on the side of the road listening to the voices and steps going by. For a moment I stared at the rags she was wearing, at her dirty face and hands, then put the doll in her wondering arms.

For an incredulous moment the swinging eyes lay still, then once again they flashed from side to side filled with rapture at the flitting things. Then she said, "You give the doll, Mrs. Henderson."

I do. "No longer blinded by my eyes."

August 2 · By now, as a result of K's firm hand and professional persistence I have at last found out how to really teach drawing. I evolved what I call a Drawing Dictionary and I was dying to try it out. At lunchtime there was a grand rubber hunt, pencil negotiations, and in the class of K's seniors in my own big room were Polly, Mando, Saul and K himself, and even Pauline was there. In the other room I had stowed away my little ones making three blind mice in plasticene, if not a hundred and three blind mice, which I knew would hold them down—first removing Jacob, of course, and young Bernard, whom no number of mice, blind or seeing, could ever hold down. I brought Pearly in with me.

The room was crowded and I gave the juniors correlative work on magpies.

For this most thrilling occasion of my appearing as an artist I wore the smock with the honeycombing to enhance the atmosphere and gave them all the drawing book to be called a Drawing Dictionary, on the first page of which we made pencil drawings evolved from a cube. Mando, who can milk a cow and is to be cultivated, and Polly were impressed to see Saul, Pauline and K drawing, Saul was impressed to see the Maori girls who had left school drawing, Pauline was impressed to see me teaching, the children were impressed to see the grownups drawing . . . that they could descend to a desk at all, let alone get in it, and I was impressed at everyone drawing. K, I felt of course, did the best drawing, while Saul was a bit at sea though I knew far better than to say so. Pauline's was stunning.

I was more than impressed—I was happy. I was clear about what I was doing, I wanted to do what I was doing, this section, anyway, of the arduous day's program was plainly working out, I had an attentive and eager audience among whom were several I loved, Saul appeared to be listening and possibly admiring—I hoped—and K was straight out proud of me and would surely praise me later if I could wait for it and not bring up the subject myself. What an hour of what a life!

And even though afterward teaching and home routine blocked the tide of impulse to draw, play and write myself, breaking wide within me—even though today I'm mad to go to Selah but must teach school instead, not wanting to dismay K or disappoint the children—even so, that hour was not without value: in it I confirmed my ability to achieve, given the opportunity, if only as a teacher.

·   ·   ·

The appeal of the Department against taking any more teachers into camp has been adjourned *sine die*—marvelous terminology—although it brings up the question of Susie again, especially with aeroplanes over the River. Perhaps Susie could be adjourned also—*sine die*—unless of course . . . Mando . . . ?

It is not true yet that where there was K walking about the grounds among his animals, children, and garden and to and fro from school there is silence and nothing but the shadow on my heart. "I never really believed you'd be taken," I said.

"Neither did I."

Saul said later when he came for his milk, "Perhaps he won't be going. How can they take teachers?"

"They've taken hundreds. There's been no word in New Zealand about teaching being a reserved occupation. You mustn't go too, Saul."

"Hell, I've hardly come."

August 8 · Into August now and spring. I made it this morning to Selah about half past nine. Checking my watch, hour by hour, each minute severely won. My watch is my rival many a time: Who wins, the time or I? Life is fast at thirty—*my* thirty—and urgent.

An hour to bring the manuka in as it makes the yard untidy, seedlings to be replanted that must have been pulled by those magpie pirates, and the bottom of the fence to be blocked to foil invading sheep. Some wood collecting too, and I picked some daffodils. Water to bring, fire to light and a brief clean-up inside: trifling jobs with a world war raging, against the backdrop of the enemy at the door, but actually bigger than war to me—the necessary fiddling of a workman indispensable to the whole. Unless I am warm I cannot work, unless I work I cannot be well, unless I am well I cannot love and unless I love I do not live . . . whereas to live is the thing in a world at war, with slaughter the key word.

An hour, ten-thirty to be exact, before I wash my hands

and settle down to gracious and dignified work, which should go without too much trouble: a soft warm day, a showery rain, few drafts, and a finger of sun. Reasonable working conditions. I can't see what more one needs to become a worthwhile person than today's conditions—few drafts and a finger of sun. "But well I know," wrote Tennyson, "that unto him who works, this grand year is ever at the doors!"

August 15 · Time is too short these days after school before the darkness comes to make a dash for Selah. Saturday bears more of a load than ever, and on occasion Sunday. Sundays are prone to bring Home Guard parades, when it's my turn to be the mother. My landings are fewer now and much more concentrated. Much more hangs on the way of the wind and whether the smoke is blowing. And my word, do I get off smartly in the morning, although I did call at Saul's for the geranium slips. He was still in his interesting dressing gown having his cup of coffee and persuaded me to join him, which the lover in me was pleased to do but the artist grudged it. In no time I was off up the road.

So fresh and exciting this walk up the road with haversack on my back. Oh, the rounding of the corners vital with fern on the overhanging banks! Rounding these corners, pausing at the waterfalls gazing at them enraptured, following the lazy-morning movement of the birds and heading for my haunted paradise, my personality changes. Off fall the wife, the mother, the lover, the teacher, and the violent artist takes over. I am I alone. I belong to no one but myself. I mate with no one but the spirit. I own no land, have no kin, no friend or enemy. I have no road but this one.

Often as I walk this road in order to use the time or to crush out some current heartache I revise recent extracts but I purposely did not this morning. After the vortex of the week at school and the whirlpool of the drama at home I needed this

gifted morning, all that it had in its pocket. I needed the serenity of the forest on the dreaming ranges and I laughed at the
way the lambs would jump all four feet in the air, while those
ewes not yet delivered chewed the sober grass. Spring is far
from exclusive but universally contagious.

At Selah the daffodils were flat out blooming, and just as I
was about to return home for my keys Jonquil called over the
gully, having followed me with them. "Look," she cried, "the
daffodils!"

"Walk between the rows, my love."

She squatted and put her face in them, then strolled erratically through the double column of yellow. So that's what
was missing last Saturday.

No blows for me today. I manured the ground for the geranium slips and brought water from the spring.

In the afternoon K came up with the children and his ax and
we all gathered wood, manuka stumps from the slopes, haul-
ing it across the creek and up to the whare.

A high neat stack on the porch now. Saturdays of promise of warmer work. And it was silky-satin heaven to feed
them in Selah: tea and scones for K and milk for the children, and it was woolen heaven to know that he approved of
my awful running away, enough to look after my interests
here. To a high degree it pacified me that support was in my
home, making me independent of outside loves. It made me
feel dearly part of him and grateful beyond gratitude.

At this moment with the fire at my back and the prospect of
many more fires from the stack on the porch, the heat of it
penetrating me is a strong metaphor of K himself.

August 20 • Over a week before the Department said so I
started the spring holidays to spend all of each day at Selah,
with breakfast and dinner at Saul's place and to work there if
cold, but first I paid a quick visit to school to fix up Fran, who

is four now, with his new book, having heard him in his re-
vision cards after breakfast, for I couldn't possibly disappoint
him. Into my own hands this book came from the cupboard
and I gave it to him as he stood in line, straight in his soft gray
clothes. With his blue-heaven searching eyes and his drive to
read, this child is my own personal affair and it would be my
hand and no other's that gave him his book which he took
without his usual "Thank you"; he looked straight ahead,
gazed rather, which I, his mother, knew to be intense emotion,
well beyond excitement.

So I got myself off with books and food thinking two
things: that anything worthwhile has its price, especially a
thing like freedom, and that surely I could pay this price without extravagant regret, a couple of days' absence from school
and home; and that teaching, I found with alarm, meant more
to me than I'd ever supposed and was sending down stiff tap-
roots into my heart.

Yet as I walked up the pretty bush road amid the spring-
green paddocks gay with irreverent lambs, my thoughts were
anything but springlike, made of Thursday crying this morning at the frequent three-cornered conflict—home, school and
"work." There was no revising in mind of the latest quotation
but an examination of how each pays bitter coin to the other:
how the home pays for the hold my work has on me, how my
work pays for the hold that teaching has on me and how
teaching pays for what my home is to me—the water hole
where the meaning springs. Where is the quotation from my
study that could solve these impassioned conflicts—a formula
for living the way I do?

Yet the sharp day may come when my center of it all goes
off to war, he the only solver of problems I know; then these
morning storms when I separate myself will be recalled, by
comparison, as milky sunshine. A relief it was to come upon
old Pop Vincent working on the road, who told me with feel-

ing about the subsidence of the road at this point and to whom I told the latest news: the combined operations raid on Dieppe when we lost ninety-five planes. Then he talked about the Allied offensive in Guadalcanal and of the thousands of troops returning from Fiji to defend our homeland and said that K would certainly be stationed in New Zealand and not overseas at all. From such casual sources comes comfort.

Out of sight of Pop round the corner I forgot the pain sufficiently to scoop a few handfuls of gravel in my pocket, and by the time I found the surviving seedlings quite high and healthy and myself acclaimed by the daffodils, the tempest within was blowing lower. After all, everything has a right to its place in life—home, school, work, lover, payment, conflict, crying, the lot; rowdy children no more in the yard of the mind to be accommodated. Enjoy the happy interludes, O my Self, when they visit you, unshadowed by before and after . . . the joyful moment now in the silence of Selah.

But as the stolen week wended through our complex life, the school haunted me worse than Whistle and Mai Mai. The children's books, I knew, would be ready for me and Jonquil told me the children missed me so I returned to school on Friday, when I saw to their books and took my fair share of end-of-term cleaning. But I returned to Selah on Saturday and Sunday, at which Saul protested, "You return only to go away again and I don't get the chance to see you."

"Oh dear," I sighed and walked off through the rain, but when I returned to get my keys and called through the window, "Goodbye dear," there was no loving answer.

It rained even harder up the road and by the time I arrived at the spot where I had hidden my billies it had no thought of abating. As I filled them with gravel I got wet in all sorts of places but the dear rain has glamour for me. Alone among the hills in the spring downpour I was so happy, though as I plodded along with my now heavy billies I did wonder if I'd done rightly about Saul, but it's too late now, I decided—besides, Saul weeps with ease.

At Selah out came the prewar colored chalk that is well off the market now, and I spent the day drawing—I drawing this time, and not just teaching. Now at the end of the day I have just completed the Water-Carrier on the wall. When Saul saw it half finished yesterday he went up close to see if it was detachable but found it stuck on for good, done on the newspaper I'd pasted on the wall and later calcimined. An excellent, oh, excellent! surface for chalk, my favorite fleeting medium. The destiny of the Water-Carrier coincides with the destiny of Suicide Cottage, whatever that destiny is . . . its audience evacuees or Japs. For better or worse it is part of Selah and no man can put them asunder. "Who wants it anyway?" I said.

"I do," petulance.

"It's a celebration of our wedding anniversary, which is today."

Well, it's finished now and even I can't see how it can be removed without sawing out a piece of the wall, which would hardly delight Mr. Snowdon, but I feel very tired after the fevered effort and am writing this waiting for the kettle to boil and for Saul to come, though after this morning I don't expect him. This recurring quarreling . . . there are times when I think I ought to get it over but what waste of sacrifice all that time till now. No, no, *never!*

Writing these nothings while waiting, talking to my Self. I'll wait a little longer for Saul to come before I make the tea. I'm very disappointed not to see him look at my finished picture. Not that I'm able to give it to him, or to anyone else for that matter, unless I hand over the whole whare too.

No one here. No one to see this beautiful girl carrying the heavy pitcher, her bare breasts touched with light; with the dusk approaching she's more alive and mysterious than before. I'm sad there's no one here to see my finished picture. I'll make the tea on my own.

September 19 · Spring has reached into September and the German Army into Egypt, yet I still found mind-space this morning and supplies of fury to give Rosie Tahore the tongue-thrashing of her life, even in terms of the River—for helping her goddamn self to my demonstration chalk well off the market for years and using most of my one stick of yellow, and though she stood still and serene throughout, my tongue only stopped when my ammunition ran out.

While the Allies face up to the Axis in Egypt we face up to the concert next week, I going in mind right through the Pied Piper play after I'd turned out the light last night, which helped neither my early rising nor the number lesson at school. "I'm worried," said K, "that your Primer Four can't add. You'll have to change your method." Which I take to be the failure of my entire number scheme. Which could well be so: my own counting is no better.

·   ·   ·

I and the spring stride bravely on in the spearhead of assault with not a thought of surrender in spite of some very cold Saturdays. It is fine and warm today though, and I expect both K and Saul are breathing sighs of relief last Saturday was a disastrous failure. That morning, feeling a shameless mother to leave her children, and a faithless wife to leave her mate, I walked out the door in my Saturday tears thinking that K disapproved, regardless of evidence to the contrary. This restraint of his on a Saturday morning . . . but could anyone blame him? After our looking forward instinctively to being together in dual relaxation earned from the week's severe disciplines—this Saturday morning parting. A heartbreaking business to part at all for any reason at all.

As I set off along the path from home, the children weeping behind, I too cried, but too pathetically I think, far too audibly, hoping to unmask K, but I got the wrong result. Almost in tears himself he hurried after me, "I send you off and you start this crying."

"It's just that I love you all."

"This won't do. You go to your work."

"I haven't been sleeping lately."

"It isn't fair for you to go on like this. Every Saturday. After all I do to help you and to get you off, even to offering you the whole weekend. Now you go and do your work." He turned on a furious heel.

The wind that Saturday was from the south and at Selah Misery met me in person. The room was continually full of smoke and I repeatedly opened the window to let the damned stuff out. But my disgrace at home burned my eyes far worse than any smoke. Misery gripped my hand and took my pen and finally Misery won.

At one P.M. smoke, cold, unhappiness, shame, disgrace and failure for the first time drove me from Selah. I decided to go home again to make my peace with K and to work in the draftlessness of the school, but nearing home I heard the voices of the Maori children shouting in the village and I turned round again. I climbed from the road over a hill to the other suicide cottage a million times worse than the first so I went to the lake below it seeking a sheltered spot.

And that's how I spent that afternoon, wandering in the cold among the valleys, reading Adler on occasion, and trying to work out what was wrong with me that I might learn to mend it. Where was the fault? What made me cry? Why couldn't I be like other wives and look after my home and family? But all I came to was a conglomeration of conclusions as thick as the smoke in Selah: it was the lack of sleep I had suffered lately, it was the irritation hounding my days, it was the loss of my ration of silence with my own children at home, others' children at school rattling on helter-skelter, I had missed my Saturday the previous week when K was on pa-

rade, the feeling of fetters on a Selah morning when we tried
to part . . . everyone's fault but mine.

The unwelcome term "self-pity." I wrestled with the word
in the cold by the lake. I fought with the infinite disgrace of it
and with impassioned aggression I flung myself against the
sense of guilt that poisoned my Saturday freedoms. According
to the book in my hands we should all meet each other in a
feeling of equality, but shame would have nothing of that.
After an hour or so by the water I changed my topographical
position.

I climbed off again over the brow of the hill and sat beneath
the manuka, where I watched the showers passing by in silent
company and the magpies in the swamp. Since they were feed-
ing I would too and I ate the apples I'd brought and fell to
picturing a Selah with a bricked-in fireplace, warmth without
smoke, where the tragedy room was bright with curtains and
beds, gracefully flower-patterned, and the front room housing
a piano; a place where a woman could retreat for a few days at
a time and where my own kind would drink wine with me.
But bricklayers did only essential war work and we hadn't the
money anyway.

Moving again to keep the circulation going I found something warmer in the lee of a stump by the tree where the orchids grow . . . if "warm" was still in my vocabulary . . .
and had another read of Adler. The idea being to rehabilitate
myself before returning home. When the shouting in the village was likely to have stopped I'd go home to a good hot
bath; I'd wash my hair, wear a scarlet blouse, wine with K and
generally erase my disgrace this morning. But it was toward
evening before I did.

· · ·

It was not until even the magpies had had enough and the
living, so personal showers were plotting dark things for the
coming night that I set off back over the hills to find the road

again where the gravel underfoot seemed so friendly and the dripping tree ferns motherly. At Saul's gate I called in to tell him I wouldn't be down this evening and I had to walk through the cottage to find him in the surgery in his white coat. He swung round surprised, "Darling!"

"I won't be down tonight, Saul."

He came close, hands on my shoulders and examined my face, plunged out of sight in my eyes. "What is it?"

Two tears replied, two only and very small, but they dug like coals.

He kissed me. Then he lit the fire in the drawing room, made the tea and read me Wordsworth.

All that was a week ago but today the weather is milder. I began work without the fire, understandably, but it turned out too cold. So I lit the damned thing after all and although I still had to go through the window-opening, smoke-letting-out sequences the wind is not so bitter, nor my heart either. Without a bricked-in fireplace Selah is not a winter resort. Strangely, the spring has been colder than winter . . . something to think on . . . but summer is supposed to be coming.

. . .

Summer is supposed to be coming, but for the time being spring is in residence sitting about in her multitude flounces of casual careless colors, and a cold guest too. The River has a habit of concocting fogs that don't shift till eleven or after, the brutish breath of the taniwha. Before nine you can hear the children coming up the hill, can hear their voices coming, but you don't see them till they're near, not until they mount the steps of the hill and emerge from behind the school; brief shadow-shapes.

They shiver, too, most of them, in their accidental clothes and with their feet bare. Bernard and his bigger sister Jane, of course, wear strong shoes, being pakehas, and some of the big girls—Josephine does—and our own three children, but most have the attitude that shoes as such are less than worth the trouble. I'm fond of bare feet myself, but not till summer and never at school.

Looking out the window through the fog I wonder in humility why they come, watching them circle the school; you wouldn't think the law could reach this far winding up the Whanganui River. If I were a child I don't think I'd come, not if I could help it, through the taniwha's breath to a teacher like me. It's astonishing that they should and it flatters me in an inaccurate way; I can't believe they actually *like* their work enough to brave the fog to do it . . . and it touches me also.

There's Kata—she's got shoes—her hand in Rosie Tahore's, unconscionably happy with her big eyes lifted in thralldom, coming round the school through the fog as though she were entering heaven, a paradise invisible. What is behind their coming? I wonder—it can't be that simple little story I told them months ago now about the teacher going away. Another group rounding the school, shivering, big and little ones . . . Holly Rowe trailing Caroline swinging her black silk plaits as though she knew what spring was for, Pearly and Huhua whose father was killed at Guadalcanal last week, Lucy and Friz who are Tiny's sisters and belong in the senior room, and some more behind them. Most of them at once. There are no clocks in the pa, so they say, yet they all know when to come. K refuses to ring a bell at eight o'clock as the former teacher did, the colonel retired from India, to give them a clue to the time. They don't really need any clue: they sort of rise like birds by instinct at migrating time.

Pathetic and touching, I don't know why. I'll give them some dancing when they come in and build up the manuka fire.

Later, with the line inspection over—health inspection they call it—after a morning word from K, and when they have marched into school to the music, Airini reminds me that although it is spring we haven't yet sung "Pussy Willow," and produces a sprig of it. So we lift our voices to "Little Pussy Willow, high up on the tree, When we see your fuzzy coat, bright and gay are we. For we know that spring has come when you first appear; Know that soon the blackbird's call, joyfully we'll hear," another English song imposed on the race. The Department could well put some shivering New Zealand artist on a warm secure salary to compose Maori school material—songs and poems and local stories. Me, for instance.

The first time Kata has heard this song about the Pussy Willow and before it is over she runs to the . . . no, she feels her way to the piano in glorious impulse and hammers the surprised keys, at which the children shriek in laughter, unnerving their audience, the magpie on the windowsill. I do not send her away for although she can't see she can hear all right and has perfect ear and rhythm. The keyboard could be her occupation while the others are having drawing, if I could stand the noise. Right on this moment, an accomplice in impulse, mid-course in this song I guide her cold fingers along the tune, which the children feel is loudly funny. "You don't have to laugh *all* the time, you might make her shy." No, not funny, they don't think it funny, it's that they often laugh in surprise, their reaction to something surprising.

"Like this, Kata. No, not the same finger every time, each finger wants a turn. This one, now this one, now this. Look, this note runs a long way up away from the others. Feel these two black keys? Now this flat key beside them, that's C. Remember that. Play it and say 'C.' "

"C! I got a C!"

"Try it again," and the tune begins to come.

"I make the Pussy Willow!" her upturned eyes elated at some vision we do not see, being blinded by our eyes.

Into some dances now which will be on the concert program, and which we turn on for visitors from the House whenever they wander this way. "Horowhenua, you stand in front of the fire, please, so that no one will tumble in." English dances, of course, not Maori, but they love these too, so receptive the Maoris to foreign cultures. You've got to admit they absorb the English culture on the periphery of the personality whenever they come upon it, which is all the time at school, but I don't think it is integration. As they lift and leap in delighted pairs in a delighted ring the steam from their breathing mingles with the fog of the taniwha's breathing, but I must study Maori legend more.

When I leave the keyboard to demonstrate a step Kata takes over behind me and the next thing we've got a choreography the like of which . . . like nothing we've heard before. Not tune as such, not what a pakeha would call a tune, but any amount of anything else, and she sings as well, at the top of her voice, grandly improvising. How lyrically happy this blind child is, more than the rest of us, and heavens, listen to the words: "I the Pussy, I the willow! I the Pussy Willow! Willow Pussy in the tree, I the Pussy tree!" Maybe we don't need the Department to put a shivering artist on a warm salary . . . we've got a free one here.

With the dancing over, the moment I have settled the others down to their morning writing, Pearly starts up on her morning crying, her morning bellowing, from the wide dark-pink loose mouth. I don't know what they did to her or who did it, but God, the din! In no time the piano lesson I was giving Kata loses and Pearly's voicebox wins. "Pearly, you've got a voice like a girl taniwha. Close that mouth and get on with your work."

"Please Ru he tread my feets."

"Well keep them tucked under the desk."

"Please my feets theys tuck unner. Ru he kick my feets unner the des."

"Sno," from Ru.

"Shess," from Pearly.

"Sno."

"Shess."

"Sno."

"Shess."

"Ru, you say, 'No, I didn't.' "

"No-I-didn."

"Pearly, say, 'Yes, he did.' "

"Yessadid."

"Now go on with your quarrel, at least in decent English."

"No-I-didn."

"Yessadid."

"No-I-didn."

"Yessadid."

The rest of the children like this rhythm and take it up themselves, from a whisper first, then in growing volume until there's a full-scale chorus-chant. "No-I-didn, yessadid." A foot somewhere taps the beat, then all the other feet: "*No*-I-didn, *yess*adid, *no*Ididn*yess*adid." Kata supplies a tune to it, returns to the keyboard and away we go . . . What on earth has happened to my teaching? All that careful preparation I did for an "orchids" topic—but if I could find time to put down on paper Kata's exploding words and music this morning I'd save the Department a risky salary, my own salary included.

After lunch, when the taniwha has ceased bitterly breathing and I return from the house in the sun, I see a line of children in crocodile formation, the hands of the one behind on the shoulders of the one before, sixteen or seventeen of them, chanting in rhythm round the school, stamping out the beat: *No*-I-didn, *yess*adid, no-I-didn *yess*adid," with Yessadid herself in person at the head and No-I-didn second. Is this the inside and outside of a Maori child married up at last? Is this integration? But K and I roared and swayed with laughter.

Fog, song, laughter and dance, tears and a piano lesson, and a stunning new pianist. Summer is supposed to be coming but spring is still in residence and on rocks another day.

October · At the first corner one morning, having left my things inside Saul's gate for the evening, I heard a step behind me and, turning, saw Saul. "Why didn't you come in? Did you think that I would keep you?"

I had no reply.

"You know that we would both have a better day after seeing each other for a moment."

Arm in arm we walked up the road for two more corners when he said, "This is as far as I can go."

"Come further," I begged, "and see the orchids."

"I saw them last Thursday."

Well come and see my Water-Carrier. She's been finished a long time now and nobody yet has seen her. I'm going to rub her out and draw something else."

"No, no, don't rub her out. I'll come and meet you to-night."

"Come at dusk."

. . .

I found my back yard had been used for docking, the fence removed, grass obliterated, the path wiped out. I cried, loud Maori crying like Pearly's that echoed among the hills amid the sheep and baffled the listening magpies, then I settled down on a log and planned the time when I would be independent of lambs being docked all over Selah, and out of reach of another's will whether good or destructive. I pictured the day when I'd buy some land and do what I wanted with it . . . until the storm within blew over.

Yet hours I had hoped for among these flowers now a stretch of pungent mud, but I picked my way through it, went inside and put in a hard day's work, although in the evening at Saul's instead of study I lay on his rug by the fire and gave in to exhaustion. But I had picked myself up this morning, and had got on with my work, which was something, and "was not cast down."

And the following week, when K heard from Mr. Snowdon of a second docking to come, and even when the real owners of Selah spoke of removing the whare altogether, I was not dismayed. I'd had my blow and had got over it. I'd begin somewhere else. In the meantime I carried more gravel, did something about the fence and Saul joined me in resowing the grass one thundering Friday. Ideas must be realized. If life amounts to more than that, ideas materializing, then I do not, so far, know it.

October 24 · Still October in spring. How do I get to Selah at *seven forty-five* on a Saturday morning? But I do. Cheerfully and happily I paddled up through the torrential rain in my red cape, barefoot in the lush wet grass, dawdling in the pools worse than Hellen. This rapturous time when I'm alone . . . kinless, landless, pure. Brilliantly the nasturtiums greeted me, they offhand about lambs being docked . . . they grow up and on. I raided their inspiration so that joy accompanied my work.

·   ·   ·

We feel that the attack of the Eighth Army in Egypt is a turning point in the war, yet here I am, president of the Institute, fiddling about with piffling knitting and all these balaclavas, packing food parcels, rolling bandages and earning funds at euchres. Can this be called a war effort? The choral speaking at school is wonderful and my infant material rewarding, but if only I could see some link between our school and the war. That we create to replace does not suffice. What we should do is create to *forestall*—*that's* the idea. But how? As I paint a brick house in the infant room I think of the buildings in rubble and ruin. The victory at El Alamein only points up our drooling back here. Mine anyway. Oh for a gun! When Sonny Boy is grabbed and tossed into camp without a day's notice K says, "I wish I were in his position."

"You talk as though you *want* to go."

"I wish I were in his position."

"There should be," from Ted Wallop at the Store, "no reserve occupations. Tom Snowdon could run all the farms round here with old Pop Vincent in tow—he knows a cow from a shovel. As for teachers, a couple of years' education lost to the kids would be a couple of years to the good. By Christ, if I could put in five years at the last war . . . And what about that Mada up there?"

"That TB job is a reserve occupation."

"Aw, don't give me that!"

K looks terrific in his Home Guard uniform, stripes, little hat and all, although no rifles have been issued yet. There are not enough rifles in the territorial camps, they said . . . *Anyway!* None of that solves my problem at school.

October 30 · Montgomery used our infantry as a spearhead at El Alamein but where is the spearhead in teaching? Even though my orgies of preparation continue for my weekly topics I still see no spearhead. Much preparation, much organization, does not spell spearhead. I see no success. What use my attractive classroom when Andrew won't come to school whenever Old Mai goes upriver? A great failure of mine that he should not want enough to make the lone effort . . . indifferent to my professional allurements. I must have been too severe with him—and once more I pull myself up.

As the spring blossoms on I begin a new beginning, a campaign to abolish criticism in school, a condition that has something to do with the spearhead. But what, I don't know. All I appear to be very good at is learning the hula from Mando. Yet I'm moved by my infant room and I think that war or no war, spearhead or no spearhead, I'll still teach when the need is over.

October 31 · Getting-dark time at Selah a Saturday later. There's no Saul to come and meet me, he being away on leave.

I carry something with me when I need it: a note from K, a piece from his letter written from Home Guard camp, some sentences from whomever I am reading, an extract or some enlightening lines of poetry, between my breasts where it is safe and accessible only to me. They all mean the same one simple thing—the need to feel the nearness of others. As for two blouses that Saul has sent me, I've got the pink one on. Comfort and communion: so close to mine are their thoughts they amount to physical contact. I can all but feel a hand on my arm and the way of the artist is not so lonely.

Before he left Saul said that my rising early in the morning at home to my books was different from work in the evening, that it was communion of a kind. He went further and said it was prayer.

Today's conclusion: new love survives on the thrill of not knowing each other—illusion, surprise, discovery . . . but when the discovery is complete love no longer lives on thrill alone but supplements itself. To survive it must find in the discovered some further store of nourishment; common interest, fulfilled need. Where this is found love widens and deepens but where it is absent love dies. To survive, love must change . . . because love is a living thing and all life changes in growth. The change need not indicate the death of love but its normal movement from one stage to another, each stage fulfilling in its sphere, from the thrill of new love to the strength of the mature. As love moves from one season to another, accept the change, my heart, without comparison, question or regret, for in its changing lies the evidence of its reality.

November 16 · A week ago we had a letter from the River Services asking the school for a concert to entertain posh visitors, but although we thought it a good concert it turned out to be a flop. The white element could barely bring themselves to clap one thing, and we were not asked down to the House afterwards for a chat and a spot. Might have been because they were all senior to us and all had this gray hair, or because at the last moment I wouldn't do the hula which Mando had taught me, in the hoheria skirt that her mother made me to prove something obscure. But the stinging slight brought us closer together as disaster does . . . if coming any closer together were possible.

November 21 · After the disorganization of the practices in November, how refreshing the school routine again. Ideas pound at me like enemy mortars all at once from every side. And Pauline brought back from Wellington the loveliest blocks and books for the children at school, and Jonquil spends hours at them and the little ones are enraptured. The disaster of the concert fades away, or would, did I not have such trouble recovering the things I lent the Maoris for that occasion. I've got back the three white blouses, but Mando's still got my skirt, Rosie my shoes and Hellen my laddered stockings.

November 23 · I've got a clearer idea of living, for what that's worth. Boiled down and bottled it seems to be a matter of organization. It's astonishing what I can do in a day, indeed, what more I could do in a day could I replace my errant dreaming time with thinking, planning and sleeping time. This drag of dreaming in our composition, at its worst in children. Yet there must be a use for dreaming, otherwise why is it there? Think of the power it generates trickling away like oil . . .

With meticulous forethought the work at school is easier and the children appear to behave much better, the running of our home and our lives is better, in fact everything's better. There is something to be said for Mrs. Blom, who does her washing on Monday, the ironing on Tuesday and the mending on Wednesday, since that's what I'm trying myself. The only disadvantage in organization is that the pace gets too hot altogether. On Sunday I flaked right out and wondered if I'd ever see school again but the thrill of getting up the wall pictures refueled me, confirming what I'd suspected before, that inspiration has bottomless resources like that spring near Selah. Inspiration is the richest nation I know, the most powerful on earth. Sexual energy Freud calls it; the capital of desire I call it; it pays for both mental and physical expenditure.

November 26 · A three weeks' absence from Selah over the school concert, but still no evidence of a second docking, neither is the whare removed. I've not touched my book over these three weeks. All I can show is a set of boring conclusions, glimpses and resolutions that infest the mind like weeds when the real plant is not doing well. All this writing what I'm *going to do*, in living as well as working, the time alone that is squandered, the *time* I spend in the entrancing world of fantasy, fattening my soul on the stolen prizes of what I want to happen. Unless I economize on my dreaming and put the savings into my thinking, what I want to happen will not happen. Without these inroads and tangents, thinking itself would take less time and it's *time* that's the big thing when you're young.

·   ·   ·

"When you grieve, Saul, you grieve like anything . . . you're a marvelous griever. When you read you forget we exist and when you work it's the same. When you love you go straight at it and when you sleep you die. No overlapping of reality and fantasy and we get this uncannily accurate choice of words in your poems."

"I thought that you thought they were no good."

I put my empty plate back on his table. "Why?"

"Because you never said anything."

"I was just waiting for an opportunity."

    ·   ·   ·

I must diet my soul to slim my mind. All these re-dedications, re-beginnings, re-springings into growth of the unkillable impulse within me . . . impressive but not a book.

I'm tired of being young.

    ·   ·   ·

Today I have no watch but there's much to be said for arranging with K that I'll be home at sundown, a poetic word for a start, something primitive about it, nearer the natural life that I often think I seek.

Today I lay on the bed and groaned aloud because when I read the words I had written they had no meaning for me . . . rather fetching little marks I had made on paper . . . and I couldn't do anything but groan about it.

November 28 · After setting out for Selah this morning I went in and had breakfast with Saul, a very sweet breakfast with him: grapefruit, bacon and toast. And he stood by my chair and I put my head on his breast while his arms were round my head and I heard his heart beating and felt the warmth and life in him. Then he begged me not to go out in the storm and lightning and thunder.

"But I want to go out in the rain. How can I see it dripping from leaf to leaf if I'm not out in it?"

So he gave me his coat and his watch and I set off into where I belong. Halfway to Selah, however, I had to return for my keys, which K passed to me through the window, and my umbrella too. Enclosing, protecting, isolating the storm. I was I . . . alone.

With my own key I opened my own door, filled the billy with water from the roof then sat on the porch and watched the show and when I went in and got down to work the words this time had meaning.

Summer is here, ushered in by rain as all seasons are. I've seen the winter through. But not again under those conditions. There's talk at home of a Dover stove before next winter but they're not on the market at present; neither is the money. I'll have to work in the school again when things are too bad up here. It's not so good at Saul's.

Or too good . . . I suppose I mean.

December 4 · December with the holidays coming up but I was never much good at waiting, let alone for holidays. Weeks ahead I'm gone. Before the calendar date habitually I dismiss myself inwardly, although my body is to be seen at school making like a teacher. I make sure of their reading and what I call number with an all-out effort, but after that we faint. We slither into free occupation from plasticene and clay down to dreaming, accompanied by Kata at the piano, feeling so friendly and pally all round, sympathetic accomplices. In my more offbeat thinking I suspect that with the dreaming ingredients of a mind worked off first, the laboring intellect would be clearer for practical application. Think of a room where we all came running in first thing in the morning to plunge into creativity! Ah . . . tense orgasm! . . . so that, detumesced, we could settle for number later. But you won't find that in my teaching scheme. The curriculum would be a wounded marine—it would die on the way to hospital. A teacher could be dismissed for such outlawry, sacked for sheer insanity. But oh, the children would love it, and the teacher be elevated. The children would love the teacher and the teacher would love the children. Get thee, Oh get thee behind me, Satan.

You won't get thee behind me, Satan? In an upset condition from an overdose of organization, snapping and growling worse than a stepmother as we confront the reading and number . . . suddenly out of the urgent hour, I took off on wings with them all—out the door, down the steps, up the road, and over the hills to the lake. There they played with the frogs at the edge of the water and I read a bit on the bank. As for the professional guilt, during the week I didn't see it . . . not in the face of the frog theme. Frogs infiltrated the number lessons and injected the reading lessons so that Satan scored a victory. It was Satan himself who revealed the spearhead in the sheath of the undermind. Even I could count this week.

· V ·

February, 1943 · Whew . . . another year!

I'm not feeling myself after all those parties but I'm going to begin again. Begin another beginning. You need to be young to be always beginning . . . I've all but worn out the word.

Begin early rising again for a start to get on with my study, get it in before the grip of home and school in the morning of the energy. This dawn at a quarter to five—it should be half past four—I mean to read Russell's *Let the People Think*, or, nearer the point . . . *Let Me Think*. During the last year practically everything I did about living was wrong. The thing is to somehow order my impassioned living so that I myself survive. Somehow avoid the frustration in it to release spontaneity which is elating to a teacher and contagious among children. And if there is anything right in my teaching, only Satan knows it. No more rages before the children, no more militant tongue-ing, if for no other reason than it disgraces me, myself as well as them. And with no more of those verbal daymares, there should follow no more of those nightmares when I take a stick to the children and flog them to the floor . . . the escape of violence from the undermind.

April 25 · Two months later, in April now, and I'm due for another beginning. Of these three great pulls in my life—

home, school and work—one of them must be first. So far this year the order has been school, work and home, yet the greatest of these is home. Unless our home is content neither school nor work succeeds. Home, work, school is to be the future rating. The large weekly projects using up my weekends that should be for my family . . . they've got to be cut down; the wall pictures cut down to one or two, the poems to strictly one. In fact, I mean to survive.

Last night I had promised to go down to Saul but I just plain didn't. There's a reason for everything. About nine there was a loud rapping on our door, tremendously uncharacteristic. A stunning entry, magnificent anger. There was a spatter of words, trembling chin, tight lips and his furious eyes full of tears . . .

June 3 · Another winter, the third since we came to the River. It's better working full out at school than half out or not at all. K and I both agree on this. When the children are extended it turns out easier than when they're allowed to idle. As for me, all this necessary external discipline is a brake on self-absorption and it immobilizes dreaming. Where is the time for dreaming in the pace at which we live in the front line of the infantry? Only the wounded have time to dream.

Dear Frannie says he doesn't like school on account of the work over there although he loves his reading. Conceivably that could be the feeling of the rest of the children. I don't like school either at times on account of the work over there. Surely I can lessen this feeling . . . handle us all more humanely.

July 6 · Eleven o'clock on a morning in July and I am not at school, like Andrew when Old Mai departs. Like him, I too resist and stay at home for two or three weeks. Not any more can I go round and round on the wheel of regularity any more than Andrew can, through the dim-lit cavern of routine. Not unless it promises sometime somewhere the expression of personal impulse. That cannot be organized. There must be allowed a place for this, whatever the organization. Whether the children can or not, I can't go on without it. In me the wheel has jammed, the fuel run out. I'll spend these pirated weeks thinking the thing out while I catch up on my home and reinforce my study. Already the spiritual indisposition has let up a little. Here I will stay in my own home until I've come to reliable conclusions.

July 31 · The end of July now. A month since I wrote here, since the time when I took that fortnight off school, giving in then under the urgencies of school and home and overwhelmed by crises, not the least of them Saul. But during that time and since, I've been reading Dinsmore and thinking a lot of an inner principle of life: the resolution to serve others, in particular K and the children, and others I love. I've been in the depths of unhappiness and trying to extricate myself, and needed something to hang onto, and this principle did give me sporadic consolation.

I haven't had my ration of silence in Selah for eight whole months on account of the cold up there. I've been working in the school most of the time and on brief occasions at Saul's. But it's more than silence . . . it's aloneness I need. The unhappiness would not have been so nightlike, the crises so nightlike, had I had access to Selah.

September 11 · Ten months since I've come to Selah and here is another spring.

In the valley and in myself. I approached with apprehension, expecting anything. The nasturtiums dead. "But they're

annuals," I said. I'll plant them again, I thought. And I'll bring
a hammer next time and take that extra wire netting off the
fence of Mr. Snowdon's, so I can use my gate. A year since
I've used that gate since the last docking. The path is covered
. . . I'll weed it. I'll keep on planting the nasturtiums, re-
establishing the fence and weeding the path. I'll just keep on
cleaning up after Mr. Snowdon. I cannot not do it.

The wood's still on the porch. No one took the wood. And
there was "Selah" still written on the door in charcoal and
scarlet lipstick.

I opened the door with my shiny key and it opened sweetly
enough. No one could have tried to break in . . . praise God
for ghosts. I went in. Everything the same. A bit untidy, that's
all. Of course children had been and the rats. One expected
some show of children and rats. Amazing, I thought, to find
it the same after all this time. Then I saw the window.

The lower pane was broken, glass lying about on the table,
and the lower clip was undone. They actually have been in,
I thought. I looked everywhere for signs. Nothing was
touched. They must have found the biscuits though. Maori
children have no morals about food unless that all food belongs to all could be a moral. The biscuits were untouched. So
I looked again at the window and the top clip was still shut.
They hadn't been in at all.

I said to the sophisticated lady on the wall, "They couldn't
get in," and to the girl there carrying the water, "They
couldn't get the window open so they couldn't get in."

At last I took off my heavy haversack and began to feel the
heavenly healing of Selah once more. Look at those daffodils
through the window. How can I board in that huge fireplace
for the new stove? So still. No voices. Only the lambs and
ewes calling each other. I'll draw a big bird on that wall and
I'll call it "My soul . . . there is a country, Far beyond the
stars . . ."

I began on the cleaning first, though—the floor, the sack

rugs, the bed cover, the table, the cupboard and wherever the rats had been. By half past three when the children arrived the bird was done, its wide wings stretching abroad the wall, and I was free in time to watch Jonquil walk through the daffodils in her blue dress again.

September 19 · Yesterday the little Dover stove arrived called the Hot Dog with its long pipe chimney. Too miraculous that I don't have to wait until after the war to get a new brick chimney. This does encourage me. Soon I'll buy a reading chair, fix the burst door of the haunted bedroom and replace in there the broken panes. Back crowding came the old dreams of a year ago: shrubs in the yard, a small water tank, new wallpaper, the bedroom done in cheerful chintz, the big front room with a piano, coffeepot, wine and lager to entertain elegant friends, someone coming across the paddock to see me . . . How I love this dream! O darling God, this must happen to me! And life is long . . .

· · ·

Now I must get down to thinking out the dreadful crisis last weekend, when for half a day I believed that the life of my heart had closed, and after that all the other crises of my ten months' absence from Selah, mainly to do with loving. Or overloving if you like. Over-everything . . .

September 22 · I'm writing in school at noon. Spring has begun a new beginning, but me, I'm tired of beginnings. I'm too tired from late election speeches to teach at all this morning. Why try to begin all over again when I growled at two children this morning? True, Olga tore up a book in her damnably nonchalant way, hid the visiting dental nurse's syringe, and Jacob wouldn't work *at all*. Not that I don't know all too brilliantly the reason of our common ills: the constant thwarting of desire within ourselves, in me and in the children. This desperate longing in us all to get and do what we *want* to do. How much longer can we stand the timetable? You'd never know from my temper that I've had a fortnight's holiday or that I'd come to a profound conclusion.

October 2 · Although the Dover stove is here in Selah, chimney and all, it is not yet in position and I've still got smoke and cold. Too uncomfortable to work adequately but oh, the *peace*. After that year of tumult, crisis and drawn out heartache. Life spare me from another year of Saul! But there's much rededication to be done, reorganization of my life, reorientation of myself, recovery of the lost goal . . . to be a worthwhile person.

But so far the present rules—the immediate plans to fix up the bedroom and paper the place. Full of wonderful plans . . . I must go to town soon.

October 5 · My October tongue got away again and so did my hand on a desk . . . disgraceful undignified performance. The tongue of a frustrated artist is a kamikaze pilot—frankly suicidal. When four of them stroll in late—Hellen, Rosie Tahore, Caroline and Mere, if you must know—and Pearly trailing after, they interrupted my elocution lesson, and I've had enough of interruptions. I told myself and them that the best is got out of "these Maoris" only when they know there's force in the background. As things went, after that the lesson ended up smarter and fuller than ever before and with far more learned, but I would rather have got it another way.

I know the real reason: the awful stress I've endured lately from so much frustration, not being able to do what I want and not enough Selah. It's the law of life that somebody pays, although I doubt if I'm ashamed of myself. I'm sick of being ashamed. I'm sick of blaming myself. I cannot, honestly . . . *always* be wrong. If only I had someone else to blame I'd take time off to do so.

Never mind, never mind. During my willful holiday I did catch up on my study and reading and in spite of the front-line action at school I've cheered a little lately. Moreover, here at four A.M. in the warm and silent kitchen with the household still asleep, hope takes another breath and opens her eyes, stretches her limbs and rebubbles like the kettle on the stove. Which is the thing about being young in the spring . . . rejuvenation, rededication, regeneration. Beginning, beginning and beginning again.

October 6 · Only the next day . . . Never would that young Bernard overlook an opportunity to exercise his art of dodging and fooling. I'm certain it was he who led the others, Jacob of course, and my own Frannie. Before I left for the house with the big girls for homecraft I had most carefully set the infant room to free occupation, all so lyrically happy, but these three reinterpreted free occupation and were throwing clay on the wall—not that it hurt the wall. It was the sullen insolence of the white one, Bernard, that didn't get by. Two white ones this time, and one brown one who stopped an earful . . . with special reference to young Bernard, the sour little criminal, the saboteur, the little fifth columnist—all of which I told him. I let him have it!

Nor am I as sorry as I should be over tongue statistics since it does make things easier on the surface, but I'm not going to do it again. For the hundredth, the thousandth, the millionth time, I admit that it all stems from me, but on account of the furious life I lead I cannot help it. For the sake of everyone else I mean to cease regretting any more inalterables. All I can do is keep on beginning.

October 19 · October shows a shift, all but invisible, to the technique emerging. I take more school time for my own work now, pirating it or merging the two. After play yesterday, with the reading and number behind us, I took flight with my entire roomful and ended up at Selah where as they played delightedly and incredulously among the raupo in the swamp and caroused beneath the trees I read Russell's *Why Men Fight*, hoping to find out *Why I Fight*. To their delighted baaing and cackling rising and echoing from hill to hilltop I read what he had to say on the life of the spirit guiding both mind and instinct. I wondered if I had entered that world or if not, would I ever? One thing was plain, however—that I was obliged to be kind to *everyone*, especially small children.

October 25 · The stove is in! After looking at it here for five weeks! I'll forgive my transgressors all their transgressions! My spirit is no longer a bird of chalk on the Selah wall but a shape, a shape flashing about in the gullies, shooting the clouds and hovering over the ranges.

Saul gave me this day. A holiday, with K on parade, he took the children. On a bed that K made in the doom room I lay and read and was quite unmoved, liking the incredibility of it. With timber and wire netting K has knocked up two of these beds in there so that some night I'll be able to sleep here in order to go to work straight from bed in the early morning, not lured by the beauty, the beauties of the day, not stirred and tempted to dream. After walking up this particular road to this exquisite spot it's hard to turn from reality to that esoteric area of the mind. All you want to do is play and plan. I need to learn to sleep here alone in order to have the early mornings here alone, so that when I feel lonely I will not be able to go to K's bed as I sometimes do but will have to find what I want in my work . . . but I think that might be beyond me. In any case I'll try it with someone else first, and that night is not too far distant.

October 28 · I am here at Saul's place trying to do some work. It is a quarter to eight and I must get back to bed soon. I am entering this because it's the only kind of thing I can do not on my own. I can't spare the time to talk . . . not midweek. I talk on Saturday nights of music—when and *if* I come.

I attended to my appearance, which is important. So far he remains my sole usher into that world of cultivation which I seek and besides . . . love must dress itself. I put on the brilliant Indian blouse in spite of his disapproval of it. I feel my wearing of it to be a symbolic act of independence. He doesn't like it but I do and so I'll wear it. He is afraid of its bold truth, too glistening and certain. It's too opposed from his careful halftones, as different from them as I am from him, as my way of life is from his. Why should I accommodate him? How much of my true self I camouflage and choke in order to commend myself to him, denying the fullness of me. How often have I paraded sweetness and interest when I felt otherwise; pretended to take careful leave of him on many an occasion when I would rather have walked right out. How I've toned myself down, diluted myself to maintain his approval.

He doesn't like this blouse, hasn't seen anything like it before, maybe . . . not in his reserved circle; nevertheless I wear it. And another thing: I mean to study tonight and not fawn on him trying to keep his love, and I'll return exactly when I want to.

·   ·   ·

Early morning at home. I'm thinking of last night still instead of doing word study. He must have sensed the resolves in me, being gifted at "sensing things." Saul stroked the blouse and said it was lovely. "You look interesting," he said. "Do you feel interesting?"

"Yes."

It was about then that, because it was my precious bedtime on which my days depend, and because I was very tired, I decided to go home. And there was not going to be all this leav-taking, so time-consuming. He would have to accustom him-self to both my blouse and me . . . the really me. I closed my book decisively, replaced the pencil in its box and put on my cardigan—perhaps it was the putting on of the cardigan that was the mistake. But he didn't look up alarmed as he should have, and I thought, He has already sensed the change in me, and at once I began to feel the price of independence . . . the hurt in him.

Alarmed myself, I went over and sat beside him at which he put down his own book. "I must slip along now, darling," I said.

"You didn't tell me you were going."

"No. But I really must go."

"What for? What are you going to do?"

"I'm going to bed."

His eyes tightened on mine like arms. "You can't go. I haven't said you can go."

I met his gaze but began to rise, at which the hold of his eyes tightened. "Have you done some good reading?"

"Yes."

I began to rise again, at which in true Mada style his eyes suddenly released mine, and symbolically he held his arms wide open, like throwing open the way out. Now I knew that the knife had struck, the wound in him deep.

He said, "Are you going to make up your face?"

"Yes, I'd better."

Sitting in the chair opposite I did my mouth, then combed

my hair in long backward sweeps from my face, feeling with distress the distance between us and thinking, This is the price of being myself. Is it worth it?

He said, "Your hair is looking better."

"Thank you."

"Are you out of clips?"

"No. I'm just not wearing them tonight."

I rose and he rose and we went to the door with my anxious arm round his middle, feeling upset at the abyss between us. He opened the door and there was a cold starry night. "Oh," I said, "it's cold," and turned to him in concern. "Now you're not coming to the gate."

"Oh . . . I *see*." The same "I *see*" of the door-slamming episode. I stood by the step of the porch, my determined exit was not going very well. Another part of me was clamoring, the loving, fearful part, clamoring that he was displeased with me. I looked up at him recalling the times when he had accompanied me to the gate with both arms tightly round me, and asked, "What are you going to do now?"

"I'll read and go to bed."

"I love you," I offered.

"Go on. Go away."

I looked astounded into his face.

Hastily he added, "I mean go to bed." Then, "You look very pretty."

There was silence that I felt should be filled but I refrained. I felt myself turning and walking away, and I thought, This is the price of being myself. I must get used to this, I must get used to walking away from Saul with pain in my heart. I must remember, I thought, going up the path, that he loves me and that this upset, far from showing that he doesn't, actually proves that he does. I tried to remember that he loved me but I didn't turn my head at the gate, not till I was on the road, and when I did I was surprised to see him still standing at the door.

"Goodnight, Sylvia," he called.
"Goodnight."

· · ·

I fretted walking in the moonlight toward the house think-ing, How could this cavern open between us after the com-munion of my holiday? But I must not worry. I must put this aside. All is well. Saul loves me. But I fretted when I got inside and K made the tea. "If these visits over the road are going to upset you—if they continue to upset you—" he said, "I'll cer-tainly stop them." And I fretted going to bed.

In the morning the taut pain was still there. Go away, he had said. I thought, I must go and see him before he leaves on his rounds. I shrank from a long day of pain with Saul down-river. I slipped away and ran across the road and down his path, through the cottage, into the kitchen, up the corridor to the surgery and into his arms. "Darling," he held me closely.

"I came for a little quick see of you."
"You naughty girl . . ."
"An impulse out of control."
"Darling, you shouldn't have."
"Do you love me, Saul?"
"I love you more. Did you think I didn't?"
"You said 'Go away' last night."
"I won't say it again. I didn't think you would feel that. I don't know you enough yet. I won't say that again."

Running home through the trees I thought, I must accus-tom myself to other people's ways . . . to Saul's ways. I must learn to live with other people after forgetting how on the Coast. I really haven't recovered yet.

November 5 · It is well over a week since I've come here to Selah, engaged as I have been in the death struggle between an ordered life and the disorder of the life of passions. I have been hurt and angry, catastrophically so, but an hour with Russell has reset me. "In their private relations," he wrote, "they are not preoccupied with anxiety lest they lose such respect and affection as they receive; they are engaged in giving respect and affection and the reward comes of itself without their seeking."

That is how I want to be: no longer enslaved by the fear of the responses of those I love to my intransigent ways. Such a formula would at least help me in the ageless issue of the conciliation between reason and feeling, if that ever has or ever will be accomplished. In the swirling plunging waters of this persistent confrontation there are times when I wish I were the homeliest housewife, or digging drains on the road with Pop Vincent.

I'll try to hold in my mind this motive—to overlook those qualities in others that hurt me and return respect and affection: ". . . an impartial contemplation, freed from all preoccupation with self, will not judge things either good or bad . . ." although God knows *I'll* never see that stage.

I must preserve my individuality and not be influenced by what others do. I must not catch their speech or their ways but keep my own. I must not resist doing what I think fit when others don't think the same; I must set and maintain my own standard . . . what*ever* of heart pain the price. I must have faith in my own judgment, my own impulses, born from the conviction that there is *some* good in me however it appears to the contrary, and that it is from this unrevealed worth that my tastes derive.

If I want to wear flowers in my hair I must not refrain because others in the village don't; and if I wish to pin a daisy on the top of my head I must not let Saul's disapproval stop me when he says it is sentimental. I must not avoid walking upright and with grace just because round-shouldered getting along is the order of the day or because a good walk draws

attention. *That* is the point! I resist abiding by my own inclinations because they draw attention to me.

I must not allow myself to be shaped by the crowd or by
the inner circle, by a husband or even a lover; by economic
molds, professional ethics or by the "accident of dwelling
place." And right now from this moment on this page, I pro-
mote myself to first-class living whether possible or not, once
and for all. Best hotels when I'm away, best trains to get away,
no clothes but good ones fashioned for me *and!* . . . no more
time than necessary among second-class people. How wonderfully bracing this is—magnificently mad! But that's it: I pro-
mote myself in hotels, trains, clothes, books, friends, enemies,
lovers, the lot. Wines and lagers too.

I must be true to myself. Strong enough to be true to myself.
Brave enough to be strong enough to be true to myself. Wise
enough, to be brave enough, to be strong enough, to be true
enough to shape myself from what I actually am. What big
words, O my Self: true, strong, brave and wise! But that's
how it is, my Self. That's how it must be for me to walk steadily in my own ways, as graceful as I feel, as upright as I feel,
with a ridiculous flower on the top of my head . . . a sentimental daisy. For therein lies my individuality, my authentic
signature, the source of others' love for me.

·VI·

November 8 · "What is your ambition, Rosie?"

The big girls and I are stringing onions over at our place one Friday, which comes under the heading of homecraft in the Maori school syllabus, and whenever we find ourselves working together with our hands like that we're inclined to be sort of chatty. Rosie swung up her gold-brown eyes and licked her wide pink lips; she's wonderful with her hands and irons the clothes better than Ruth and almost as well as I do.

"Please . . ." a pause and thought, then, "Please I might not go on going to school till I'm sixteen like Rosina. After when I leave school it might be necessary to get a job and do some work . . . A job is the same as working. I want to go up to Auckland and stay with my sister in Auckland; she's working as a nursey and she got a good work to do. My sister she gets lots of money where she working and now she got a radiogram. I expect to get one like that after when I leave school.

"I want to work in a fish shop in Auckland because it might be quite a few peoples who go where I want to work. Please work is for you to learn an you got to know how to handle when you work in a shop an tha's how my sister she got a job because she can handle. When I go to work in the fish shop all I have to do is peel all the potatoes when I start there. I will get more money or less an if I get less I won't work any more. I want more money when I work in the fish shop in Auckland, more than my sister she gets.

"But my parents they won't let me go to Auckland yet because they want me to work in some place where they want me to work and my ambition I want to go and work on my living. So my parents they are going to get me to work here in the village at the House in the kitchen or the laundry.

"But I don't want to work here because somebodies he might take me to a dance at the pa and I don't come home till morning. My mother she said, 'Get some job to learn; you just running up and down the road to school doing nothing, you won't get any money that way.' An she said, 'You get a job after when you leave school instead of sitting down and reading, for other people to bring you food round the table, you won't get any money that way. You get a job an keep going an get lots of money an work on your living.' Please tha's my ambition, M's Hen'son."

.   .   .

True, we did manage to get Rosina off to college this year, I don't know how, but she didn't "go on going to school until she was sixteen" as we hoped. As it happens we got a letter from her this week:

DEAR MR. HENDERSON,
Please forgive me for leaving college after all I say. You went through a lot teaching me which was a waste of time. This is my reason I told lies at college and was told off many times.

I did like college when I first started then I got a bit sadded when I left your school. When I came out of court I stood at the door thinking to myself I've caused a lot of trouble. I said to myself I'm sure this court case will affect the school and my Parents and college. It gives them a bad name.

Well Mr. Henderson I hope you will forgive me. Before I

go any further I would like to thank you and Mrs. Henderson for the most wonderful experience yous gave to me even though it was a waste of time. Give my regards to Mrs. Henderson and please thank her for everything she done for me, and thank Mrs. Henderson for what she taught me.

Well Mr. Henderson I hope you will forgive me. Until I hear from you goodbye and thank you very much for what you have done for me.

My regards to you,
ROSINA

Rosina's letter came up from the Store with another from Mere across the river, who was supposed to lead our action song team in a performance at the House for the guests:

DEAR MRS. HENDERSON,

I am very sorry to say that I cannot attend action song practice this morning owing to a bad reputation of pneumonia. I am very sorry to let you down at the last minute but in case I won't be at the concert tonight I would kindly advise you to choose another leader to lead the two hakas I lead. I am now on my hands and knees hoping that something quite remarkable will happen and that I would improve my sickness so that I could come and lead our action songs and hakas, for your sake, Mrs. Henderson's as well as my own. However I would truly hope that you will find a leader as good as I am or even better, It may not be too late.

May God stand beside you tonight in the action song lines and I must say, Good luck to you all. I shall keep my fingers crossed all day and tonight, and all tomorrow until I hear what happened. Thank you,

MERE

Lilac is Bernard's sister in the senior room, a pink and white and mauve pakeha. Fortunately for our Jonquil, who had been lonely for her own kind before Lilac came.

Jonquil said to her father at the tea table, "The Maori children don't like Lilac, Daddy."

"No?"

"No."

"Why not?"

"They say she's too bossy."

"Do they like Bernard?"

"Oh yes. He's not bossy even though he's a tell-tit."

"Do they like Shallcrass? He's very fair."

"Oh, quite a bit but he's really a Maori."

"Do they like you?"

"No."

"They don't?"

"They won't have *me!*"

"Why not?"

"Well, you see it's because I'm friends with Lilac. And because I'm friends with Lilac they don't like me because they don't like Lilac."

"Do you like them?"

"I *would* like them, Daddy, if I knew they liked me. But they don't like me because I'm friends with Lilac. D'you know what I'm going to do? I'm going to pretend I'm enemies with Lilac and take up with the Maoris, then when the Maoris like me I'll pull Lilac back in. I think she'll come back in. Then the Maoris will like Lilac because they already like me and I happen to be friends with Lilac. See what I mean, Daddy?"

"Yes," he said.

"I wrote a note today to . . ."

"So it was you who wrote that note in class?"

"Yes, I wrote that note. I wrote it to Lucy Rangihu making out I was enemies with Lilac."

"Does Lilac know you're going to be enemies?"

"Not yet, Daddy."

"Are you going to tell her you're only pretending, Jon?"

"Oh no. But I think she'll come back in after I'm friends with the Maoris. Once I'm friends with the Maoris and friends with Lilac too, then the Maoris will like Lilac because they're

friends with me and I'm friends with Lilac. And Lilac will like
the Maoris because she's friends with me and I'm still friends
with the Maoris. Then we'll all be friends. See what I mean,
Daddy?"

"Yes. And when did you think all this out?"

"Oh, I lie awake at night wondering how we can be friends
with the Maoris."

·   ·   ·

"Lucky, ring the bell, please."

No answer.

"Lucky," K lifts his voice, "ring the bell please. Lucky?"

"Pleasesir he's not here," from Horowhenua.

"I beg your pardon?"

"He's not here sir." Horowhenua salutes in the way they
got from the other teacher before us, the pukka sahib from
India short of an army.

"That's better. Where is Lucky?"

Salutes, "Please outside sir."

"I beg your pardon?"

"He's outside sir." Salutes.

"Must you salute me all the time, Horowhenua? This is not
the army."

Salutes, then blushes. "Sno," then in confusion, "No sir."

"Well, please go and tell Lucky to ring the bell, there's a
good man."

"Pleashess—yes sir."

After a moment Horowhenua returns, "I can't find him
sir."

"Have you looked in the trench?"

"Yes I looked in the trench sir. Only Caroline is in the
trench—with Shallcrass."

"What are they doing in the trench?"

"Pl—pl . . . nothing sir."

"What do you mean, nothing? They're not in the trench for *nothing*."

"Sir," from Bernard at hand, "Shallcrass is pulling Caroline's plaits."

"The trench was not dug for pulling plaits. Tell them to get out of it and play somewhere else, and while you're out, Bernard, please find Lucky for the bell."

Harriet sitting in her desk at the back of the room speaks; she has always had a curl for Lucky to pull and knows everything about him. "Mr. Henderson, Lucky is not at school. He's home."

"You could have told me before, Harriet. Why is he home?"

"Because." A tear on the very pretty face.

Lucy Rangihu supplies, "Sir, Lucky he got the TB sir."

"Is that true, Lucy? How do you know?"

"Sir, Dr. Mada said, sir. Dr. Mada he said Lucky he got the TB. Dr. Mada."

When K went down after school to see Lucky at the mailcar man's place, the man who reared Lucky, he said to him, "I'm sorry about this, Lucky."

"Just a bit of a cough, sir. Dr. Mada shouldn't put me in hospital just for a bit of a cough, sir."

"If the doctor says so, it's best for you to go, Lucky."

"Sir, I'm Unlucky now. Not Lucky."

. . .

K said to me after tea one night, "We'll have to part with Kata, I'm afraid. Get her off to the Blind Institute in Auckland. I'll see the Pongas about it on my way down for the mail tonight."

"She's doing all right here, dear. Learning all sorts of things. The other children teach her."

"She'll be taught more up there. We haven't got the equipment here. Braille and such things."

"Well, before you do anything wait till Saul brings her back from the eye specialist. You never know . . ."

When Saul brought Kata back I asked him, "What did he say, what did he say?"

"He said, 'She can't see and I can't make her see.' "

.   .   .

"Please Ru he fell backards into the trench an . . ."

"Stop that please-ing, for heavens sake, Tai. I can't stand any more of it. I call you by your name, don't I? You call me by my name or don't speak at all."

"Mrs. Hen-*der*-son, Ru he fell backards into the trench an . . ."

"Don't say 'Ru he fell'; say 'Ru fell.' Now start again."

"Mrs. Hen-*der*-son, Ru fell . . ."

"Never mind the *der*-son. Just plain Henderson."

"Mrs. Henderson, Ru fell backards into the trench an . . ."

"Backwards."

"Backwards."

"Spell it."

Tai looks unhappy but he spells it and, taking a big breath, starts again slowly. "Mrs. Henderson, Ru fell backwards into the trench and broked his neck."

"Not 'broked.' 'Broke.' "

"Broke."

"Well, why don't you bring him in? Fancy leaving him outside all this time."

A bodyguard brings Ru walking into school and I never saw a straighter neck, but he is yelling flat out, "Ow, ow, ow!"

"Not 'ow,' " I say. "The sound 'ow' does not occur in either the English or Maori language. That sound is actually a diphthong—ah-oo. Two sounds run together: ahoo. Stop yelling 'ow,' yell 'ahoo.' "

"Ah-oo, ah-oo . . . ah-oo-oo!"

"Good. Now show me your neck."

. . .

"What do you know of Joan of Arc, Caroline?" from K in an end-of-year test.

"She was burnt with the steak, sir."

"Now Ru, what is the name of these ranges round here?"

"The Himalayas, sir."

November 11 · One four A.M. I read from Russell, "Some degree of hardship is not objectionable as a test of the strength of the creative impulse and as an offset to the peculiar joys of the creative life." What a beautiful thing to say. So kind. Ointment on the inflammations of my teaching helping me to feel better about the conditions, feel less persecuted. The passage made me feel benign . . . detumesced. Together with the reorganization of my life at home, from which I get more time for my work, it recovers for me a dash of my native temperament, a proportion of which got lost somewhere on the beaches, in the nadirs of the Coast . . . my old lightheartedness, surviving splendidly the flood tides of denial of my creative impulse and of my lover. Perhaps the growling at school will stop and its sequence of violent nightmares. The children might even come to like me over there.

To teach much better than I do should not be too hard, there being so much on the bad side, so little on the good. Areas and areas, acres and acres of land to be reclaimed, of space for cultivation. Without going for Olga for hiding my precious prewar brush, without slathering Jacob for playing up the moment my back is turned, without storming at Pearly for tearing up her book, and at many others of them for trampling their books underfoot—I *can't stand* that!—and for not cleaning up after themselves or doing their tidying-up jobs, and at Hellen for coming late, without suspending Rosie Tahore from concert practice, without dismissing Josephine for making love up the road at lunchtime, without little faces looking in terror on mine and, above all, without all this up-roar of exploding rage, without the escape of violence in my nightmares . . . there'd be much more room to teach much better.

Now it is getting different. Now that I'm happier it is different and so is the school different, and this afternoon I go to Selah . . . actually go to Selah.

November 12 • But although I planned to leave at three-thirty; it being Friday it was homecraft with a three-week ironing and very few girls: Rosie at Raetihi missing school, Mere and Harriet on the other side of the flooded river, Hellen planting sweet potato and Caroline with a sprained wrist from making love at lunchtime; then tea to leave pre-pared for the family, my haversack to be packed with books and kindling wood and leave-taking from the children . . . so I didn't get away on time.

Hurrying up the road in the rain I reflected on my position in my small vital circle and my influence on them. It tells only too vividly on my family and Saul. When I'm unhappy my sorrow and violence cast all about me and everybody pays, right down to the baby, whereas now with my impulses back in their normal channel, now that I am happy, the school alone is different and our home—at least my home—is incredibly joyful. Though I can't say that of Saul's.

I am aware of how much I mean to each one: K, Jonquil, Frannie and Dannie, and Saul too. For some reason that is ob-scure to me they all turn to me and seek my love and I pour on them *thousands* of kisses. Except when at Selah, my body is not my own. My mouth, my face, my waist, my breasts, my hands . . . sheer common property. I'm the only one to see K's garden, the only one to walk round Saul's; I'm the one without whose goodnight kiss no one will go to bed. At this time I'm first with them all. Why does each need my love so much? You'd think my elusiveness in continual slipping away would lessen their call on me.

What a time of life this is—thirty-one years old. How long will this last? I wonder. It was not always like this in the past . . . so shy in my adolescence, so apart in my childhood . . . and cannot always be. Some day I may be looking back on these days when arms were endlessly round my neck, my body seldom my own; some day I may find myself sitting at a table with all the silence I want, possibly more than I want. There may be large echoing rooms and corridors, and stairs and stunning views, none of which would put its arms round my neck and want to make love to me, call to me in the night, unless I'm like Mando's mother smothered under with the kisses of grandchildren—what grandchildren are for, I suppose. A woman's arms need never be empty.

Now that I feel better, temporarily, I must honor all this love by trying to be gentler and kinder, by forgiving more readily and teaching more sensitively. Love has the quality of informing almost everything—even one's work.

November 13 · A wonderful Saturday morning, early and all, wasted, lost from work. I'd been making such progress, but I've been very much upset again. On the face of it I did not think it was truly my fault, but at heart I admitted that any trouble that comes to me originates in myself, and to Saul I deliberately took all the blame, trying manfully to return respect and affection, but even the beauty and silence of Selah cannot qualify the pain . . . it is here for all to see; the bird on the wall, the Water-Carrier and the sophisticated lady. Sitting on the step when I arrived with a daisy in my hair I did a whole lot more loud Pearly crying, for there's no hope of my becoming a worthwhile person. That joy I had found last week—where had it gone? "I'm not surprised," said K, "that Saul should be bitter. After all, what does he get out of this? The day you get over him, dear, that day will . . ."

"I can't help feeling he has no one. It's so little I can do."

K spoke heatedly, "You can't judge him the same as us. If he's never had anyone he'll hardly miss anyone. Not as you would, always used to love. And anyway—why should he get married? He has a home and a job and a car and independence and he sees more of you than he would of any wife. A wife would be a blasted nuisance."

I cut some toast.

"If one of us went the other would be lost, but he feels no loneliness of loss."

"I go largely because I'm sorry for him."

"But fancy being sorry for him and pitying him."

. . .

That happiness last week . . . where has it gone? But it has not all gone. The fundamental condition endures, which is freedom increased . . . freedom held, wept for and torn from the maelstrom of living. Moreover—is this, however embittered, not just another change in the growth of love, a further season? Shortly I packed my things again in my surprised haversack to give back the day to K. Walking back down the road through the wind in my pretty red smock I put more flowers in my hair, orchid and clematis, as well as the daisy.

"*He's* got all *he* wants." Pauline had said that, too. He gets all the sleep he wants, lies in as long as likes, does what he wants to when he wants to—*if* the wretch wants to which he doesn't . . . eats in peace, takes as long as likes over a meal, reads the paper after dinner . . . all that time he's got. *God!* If only I had that time . . . that opportunity . . .

. . . walking back down the road to a man who never tries to hurt me, who looks after me . . . flowers in my hair; orchid and forest clematis.

. . . and he knows exactly how to upset me so that I can't use what time I've got. Look at me now . . . coming away from Selah on account of him. He meant this. Loves to wreck my Saturdays . . .

Wild orchid and forest clematis.

Well, as usual, I called in. When I appeared in his surgery he was mixing medicine and his hair was brushed. He turned in surprise.

"Hullo, darling. You're home early."

I stood and looked at him.

He came and put his arms round me. "Have I hurt you, darling? What was it? I have hurt you. Tell me."

Tears . . . three or four.

He stroked my hands and hair. "I didn't mean to hurt you. You know that. No one can wittingly hurt you."

"I believe you, since you say it."

"I'm not cruel. I wouldn't deliberately hurt you. I'm not cruel."

"I believe that too . . . since you say so."

Not without pride, "I've messed up your day. You mustn't waste your time being miserable. I love my darling. I love you best in the world. You know that. You know how much I love you."

We had a cup of tea, he watching my eyes, but I couldn't meet his.

"You're still sore," he said.

"I'm merely groping for the cosmos to recover my perspective. I must go now."

"Go? What for? No. Stay here and have a lie down."

"No, no, I don't want to lie down. I'm not one of those lie-downers."

"What are you going for?"

I wanted K but I'm always wary of saying that. "Oh, I've got a few things to do at home."

"What things? What are you going to do?"

It came out. "I'm going to find K and do whatever he is doing."

Which I did and we had a hilarious time together. I went round his garden with him and when he milked Susie I lay on the grass beside him where Saul found me when he came for the milk.

November 15 · The utter contempt of the Maoris for any manner of property, especially expensive books. I can't stand a book on the floor let alone tramped on; enraging enough, but the innocence of offense on their serene faces as they walk upon them—that's the brick wall. And their blackboards and dusters all over the place and the irreplaceable chalk . . . how could anyone stand it? They only pick them up because I say so, not because they value them. On behalf of the culture, I was sufficiently offended to actually enjoy myself as I told them what I thought of them. Glowing metaphor! Brilliant epithet! But I needn't have made them cry like that . . . may life forgive me. To repair the ravages I'll go to school earlier tomorrow.

Yet, believe it or not, school is very much better than it was. I'm content now to teach with all my best during school hours, without half my mind blacked out, so that there's indisputable improvement in much of their work, excepting of course, number. Our overall happiness seems to arise, mine and K's, from sound foundations after all those reconstructions, re-beginnings, realizing at last as we do what's most important: the expression of innate impulse, at least some of the time, regular periods of quiet and solitude which is the water on the lips . . . occasional deep breaths of personal freedom.

And another thing. K said at breakfast the other morning, "Workbooks. The more we go on filling up these workbooks, the more I feel we are slaves to tradition. A workbook is useful only insofar as it serves the teacher."

"And a record for the inspector."

"But there are more illustrative records for an inspector. Let him talk to the children, see their work."

After all those years before, chains struck off. No more workbook! "Naturally," he went on, "we'll go on doing them. We are, after all, servants of the State."

· · ·

After the vital speech lesson, of course, this morning I and the whole outfit flapped our wings, sighed inside-out, rose, flew, lifted, soared and landed skidding on the riverbank and sighed there outside-in. An exercise in common impulse, and in the afternoon after dawdling worse than Hellen or Jacob up from the river again, settled down to a river project: boats at the pier, canoes, Pearly's wet clothes, people at the Store, guests at the House, poplars marking the graves, the trees upside-down in the water, ducks on the wing, while I worked at the piano on the concerto for easily half an hour . . . all from the achievement of atmosphere. Maoris are admirable fellow artists to share a studio with. No tongue swung loose today; besides it was lovely and peaceful without Pearly, who had gone home to dry her clothes. As for the crayon drawing of the poplars, mine, done on black school paper, I slipped in to Saul's on the way home—he was out on his rounds—and pinned it on the wall in his bedroom.

Love . . . laziness . . . art. "I have some hopes," from Russell, "of laziness as a gospel."

November 16 · Still in November. With summer returned and the days getting longer I'm moving off successfully after school again, more time here at Selah. I've really had enough of working in the school all winter, after school as well as on Saturday and Sunday, the tall-ceilinged old room with its teaching overtones still echoing from the week, and the invisible presences of the children lingering . . . no memory so powerful as that of children. You need to get away from the place. Next winter with the Dover stove in, it must be different. Of course the wood has to be cut much shorter and stoked more often, although one of these days I'll bring some coke, war willing, haversack permitting—but smoke, drafts and cold are a thing of the past. A big thing in my work.

I got away at three-thirty today and have been reading Russell's essays. The man writes simply and is accessible to me and his prose has this excellent balance. The master of reason stumbled after by me, a master of unreason, which would be pathetic were it not funny. I was going to face my book again, pushed by life's real drama, but have forgotten to bring the draft so I can't write the chapter I prepared during the first term and haven't touched since. But I'll still put my face into my poor little chapter that I've been working on lately, and does it need courage! In any case I'll have to. I might just as well accept whatever I find there, bad or good, since I can't do without my work. There cannot be anything else for me now.

At least our home is relaxed and happy, each trying to give what is important to the other. For me, from three P.M. each day until six-thirty next morning I theoretically belong to myself alone, out of which I take my sleep—if any, what with love and waking babies. As for the weekends: "How much time," K asked, "would satisfy you?"

"Just a day. Just one day. That's all I ask."

"I could give you two. Saturday and Sunday. When I am not on parade."

"No! I just want one. I wouldn't take two of your days."

"When I'm not on parade I'll give you them both."

"I do love you. Oh I love you!"

He said he understood and that he would do all in his power to help me get to my work. Indeed I have everything: health, the children, K, a home, a job and time and silence enough to pacify the raging artist. Life is all too wonderful a place as well as everything in it—I wish I could add "everyone" in it; that weekend of hell in September when Saul appeared to be less interested in me, than which no graver offense can be committed. "I can enlist now, I suppose," he had said . . .

Even cooking and dishes, teaching and mending, washing and ironing clothes gleam with the maddest glamour; even hoeing the onion patch and spraying potatoes, everything short of milking Susie, painted with a brush of stars . . . fluorescent, incandescent, iridescent. I mean to draw more again now, and paint, to get something to endure; model in clay and get back on the piano, to the Beethoven that has been waiting. Give back all that has been given to me by life. Have I found instinctive happiness? Indeed I'm almost too happy consistently. I feel like a waterfall on the roadside cascading day and night. I feel like an orchid in the fork of a tree, a magpie in the swamp. I want to share what I am and what I have with anyone who currently loves me.

How long can this last? Does it matter? "Now" is the real time. Don't let the past and the unknown future clutter the simple "now." Live true and deep, O my Self, fast and hard, the effervescent life that is "now." Crowd out the curse of fear, the remorse looking back, the concern looking forward . . .

So . . . twilight falls. An hour ago when I had a break and a smoke looking at the hills and sky I thought that if ever I built a house on the River or reconstructed Selah it would not be in spite of the rain but because of it. I and the rain get on.

So . . . I can almost face the War Institute on Wednesday . . .

November 19 · Friday. From twenty to five this morning, I made a big day to get here on time—if "big" will do for what I mean—seeing the hours ahead of me as an Everest somehow to be climbed to get here to Selah, but when I did finally extricate myself from school at three-thirty—I'm always putting down the time, I notice—at three-thirty, disappointed at being late, I found I'd forgotten my keys and had to return for them. Bloody bloody damns! In any case I had carried a haversack of coke and ended up too tired for anything. All I could do was to read Russell and think.

I find this man refreshing emotionally. He untangles my tearing struggles, the convulsions that erupt between feeling and reason, between what I obviously should do and what I madly want to do. With clinical medical fingers he examines my wounds, with speed and painlessness cuts off the dead skin to clear the discharge and binds them with antiseptic dressings of a kind unaffected by wartime shortages. The thing stops throbbing, cooled.

Although I do find "Current Tendencies" heavy weather, not really being a clever person, propelled by instinct rather than brains, seeing by feeling rather than logic.

Lately has been a great changing and turning place for me, realizing the releasing things my master teaches: the waste of emotion on trivial misfortunes alongside the potential of greatness in the mind; to think bigly enough to raise my head above the waters of circumstance to see and receive the flowers of life, to reflect the magnitude of the universe . . . in short, in my words, to be happy.

My serious failure at this time of effort is failure to forgive myself for my varied offenses, to forget them enough to recover my self-respect; to pick myself up and go forward again to be a worthwhile person, "not to be cast down." I have been only too torn with the big inner conflict of loving two men, of

both hating and loving teaching but one must . . . I mean *I*
must . . . dispense with these to conserve energy, to live to
capacity. I still need to regroup, reorganize.

"To have general peace," writes my master, "there must be
peace at the very heart, from a knowledge that you are doing
right . . . however disturbing the outer consequences of that
doing may be. For whatever the storm and tears that may be
the outer price of inner satisfaction they must always be less en-
during, less ultimately powerful than the consciousness of being
true to one's design. Be brave when its light is hidden, and find
it again. And the light will gain strength from the attention,
enough to pull your eye back to it of its own accord."

Have I the courage? I'll help myself with a vow—a twenty-
four-hour vow, and the recollection of K's last letter written
from Home Guard camp: "I love you for what you are; for
your strength and for your principles."

After that concentrated think I feel a good bit better, I've
finished playing a role. Now I'm *me*. There's been an incredible tendency in this last shaking year to imitate those I admire. God Almighty, I saw it! Patterning myself on other
people . . . where would I get and what would I be? A car-
bon copy of other people? I'm determined to stay how I am
and be damned. So! Now I'm me.

What is it that drives me to work? Is it really loneliness for
my own kind that makes me enter this diary? Individual experience cannot but be lonely. But I like thinking. It's exciting.
Things happen.

But I've had enough for the moment. The ration of silence
has done its work moving among the alarmed patients of my
nerves like a figure in white persuading them to settle.

I'll dig.

·　·　·

When I finally left for home with my books I didn't fret about leaving the children with K but found myself marveling, "I'm *allowed* to be happy."

December 5 · Another summer brings to the valley visitors whose most innocent presences upset the balances of relationships that pulse along during the year—plunge and heave and toss along, I should say. Three weeks since I've come to Selah of crises mounting and resolving themselves like rainstorms from the ranges, stealing upon us unawares to assault the valley, leaving behind them their casualties. Although the latest and most innocent of these wreckers of balances is coming to meet me later, I am actually heading hard for home to help K spray the potatoes . . . a necessary rear guard action.

· · ·

When K said, "I won't stand any more of that," I had the impulse to flare up but I've been studying and reading too well lately. The reproof was deserved after my show these days. I'd better take his authority however humiliating, recognize his ruling in his own house. Besides, he is my man and they are scarce now. In a way it's a privilege to submit. It was hard not to defend myself but since I've been misbehaving like a child I might as well take correction like a child. Although I couldn't keep quiet forever. After tea I had to say, "Have you still any doubt as to who is master of this house?"
"Doubt?"
"Yes, doubt."
"I have no doubt whatever."
I paused. "Who is, then?"
"We both are."
"Oh no, we're not."
But he went on with his reading.

. . .

Saul's nastiness is jealousy of my attention to his guest, Dr. Nankivill. When I called in on Sunday morning on my way to Selah he said, "Go and have your tea on the end of Doctor's bed."

But I took it out front in the sun where the love-in-a-mist grows, picked one, gave it to Saul and said, "Love . . . in a mist."

"What mist?"

I touched the green fronds hiding its blue. "This."

"Do you love me?"

"Yes. Why . . . have you doubted it?"

No answer.

"Why have you doubted?"

"Oh . . . I never know what you're going to do. I can never be sure. I don't know enough about you yet."

"I have more faith than you have," I said. "I haven't doubted for a moment that you love me." But I have. I'm a liar.

Eyes and hands touched and the pain in me miraculously went but at the gate he was withdrawn again—because Dr. Nankivill is to walk with me once more while Saul is on his rounds.

December 17 · I ran away here yesterday. Jonquil slept with me in the doom room. Ghosts haven't a chance with Jonquil about. We even knocked up quite a happy time except that the mother in me was depressed this morning about her wheezing since that last bout of flu. But I'm resting today because it's my birthday and a rest is my birthday present to myself. I'll read today and write tomorrow.

Yesterday I went walking again with Dr. Nankivill, maybe

again today. He said he can't book a berth back for weeks on account of the strike. The weather excels itself in sun and wind and exciting warm rain.

December 20 · Crying again. Over him. Over a love, of course. With Delia staying at our place his love no longer equates itself with me, interflows. I will try to stay here on my own at Selah for the rest of the week, until Friday night. Only K I want to see and the children.

Jealousy makes me lonely and nervous and not myself. I cannot wholly banish it but surely I can curtail its dominion in my mind, cram it out a bit. And the nervousness that painfully accompanies it I must deal with, at least lessen it to bearability, otherwise I am not myself and I *must* be brave, true, strong and wise enough to be myself. I know a cure for this vulture at heart—wring its bloody neck.

Later, seven-thirty P.M., I've applied a little cure. I've drawn the chalk vulture. Also I've made some color characters of the personae in this drama: the ones I love, the one I hate and the one I am jealous of . . . symbolic designs of their minds, and I've written on the sheet, "Five people . . . who are they?" I'll never tell them but they'll know. Yesterday at a Maori party at Mando's place Dr. Nankivill said, "Something happens here every day." Something else will happen when I show them this.

Summer night approaches. Can I stay alone tonight sharing a room with ghosts, hobnobbing with Whistle and Mai Mai? The worst jealousy cannot make me. Give me any hell of the human heart to a night spent alone with phantoms. The moment I see that sun go down I'll return and sleep with K.

January 25, 1944 · That was way back in December. The big gap in my record here is the time Delia took Saul. Well, I must

let her have him. What difference does it make to the eons
gone by and the eons to come who has him? Schreiner says,
"Humanity is an ephemeral blossom on the tree of time," for
us to use as an anodyne to pain. So . . . it doesn't matter.

And if my guts contract and I pale with loss, if when Delia
went to tea with Saul on New Year's Day I hung on to the
tank stand, saw my brown legs and feet and my white shorts
and thought how lovely they were, and said, But he doesn't
see them; if I saw my whitened knuckles on the piping and
thought, He doesn't touch them; if I lay prone on the grass
with my face in it and my fingers gripped at it and tore it
up . . . then that's one of the images to be dealt with; it
doesn't, it cannot, matter. If it did I'd die.

January 31 · Another week and the last day of January, the
last day of schoollessness. Last year has turned into a new one
and I wish I could say that my life has turned into a new one,
that I could write pages and pages about a wonderful holiday,
six weeks of glamour and bliss, but the truth is that although I
am happy this morning—temporarily—those weeks have
spelled out several hells, in particular one of the last few days.
And they all evolve from my dependence on the love of
people, on whether this one loves me or that one loves me—in
itself arising from my poor concentration, I think, my inordi-
nate disposition to dream wherein I achieve the thing I have
lost, from inefficacy of intellectual discipline. If my existence is
not to develop as a series of killing hells, then I *must* learn to
manage my mind. Must somehow undo some thirty years of
intellectual meandering, of wild nomadic thinking; must get
over those years on the Coast. At least I have taken one step
toward this recovery: I realize that my hells are my own business and no one else's fault. So I'll recommence study and
practice persistent concentration, the control of association
. . . but oh, how my soul spurns discipline!

So much for my mind, but my heart I will fill with K who has always loved me and always will and will never hurt me; "You have shown me lately," he said, "that you love me."

"Why don't you get tired of me after all these years?"

"You're too beautiful."

·VII·

February 1 · Today we begin school, February the first on the dot. It is half past four in the morning and I am with my books but I'm really so glad of school. To be candid I want to hide in the routine I so often malign, for six weeks of summer on the River, of intricate love crosscurrents, of the exercise of the heart beyond its capacity, leaving it stiff-muscled, immobilized, six weeks of impulse uninterrupted, proved too much for an advocate of it. Too much time to do what you want, too much time to dream in swimming, far too much time to swim in dreaming, whereas there is, I've found, a limit to both swimming and dreaming, a limit to the value of it. I'm relying on these naughty children to throw me a lifeline in the water, to haul me back upon the bank of reality, back into the drafty halls of reality. Moreover I like my salary.

· · ·

School saves me. Though yesterday morning I cried again. Maybe I will again this morning. I could supply any number of valid reasons why I weep in the morning when you're supposed to smile in the morning. Clearly, past thirty youth is over so that when Saul came for the milk this morning and said, "What are you crying for?" I answered, "I'm weeping for my youth."

. . .

We didn't stay too long in reality yesterday, in its drafty halls, once we tasted school. We sang every song we'd ever learned before bracing ourselves for reading, let alone number, but that was expecting too much for a first morning. Reciprocally sympathetic, we settled for a story and the longer I could make it the better, the more unreal I could make it the better, for the white ones mainly who knew the culture and for my own Frannie in particular.

. . .

Now I once knew a boy called Frannie. He was only four but he could read a book. This boy he could read like anything. He liked to sit on his mother's knee when it was cold and raining and read her the goblin story. It was about a goblin with a purple cap and he would read it right to the end.

But one day as he sat on his mother's knee reading the goblin story he didn't read right to the end. You know why, little ones? Because this goblin in the picture talked. He looked up at Frannie and said to him, "You let me out of this picture."

"Oh no," said Frannie, "you can't come out. You've got to stay in the picture."

"I'm tired of being in the picture," said Goblin, "and I'm tired of being in this book. You read this story far too often, and always read to the end. You keep on reading about me every time it rains. How would you like to be read about every time it rains? Right to the very end? And be put by your bed at night? I want a rest from being read about, so please let me out."

But Frannie answered, "I can't let you out, little Goblin, because I've only read half the story."

And Mummie said, "I can't stand only half a story; I must hear it right to the end."

Then Goblin said, "But I can't stand being read about all the time right to the very end. Not without a rest."

So Frannie said, "If I let you out for a rest will you come back in the book again?"

"I promise and promise and promise."

"And don't you be too long over this rest," said Mummie. "I'm dying to hear the end."

So Frannie got off Mummie's knee and took the book outside and he opened it at the page where the picture was and gave it a little shake. *And*—you know what, little ones? *Out flew the little goblin!*

He flew away as fast as he could and hid in Daddy's garden where Frannie could no longer see him, so he went back inside to wait. But Goblin didn't come back when he'd had a rest, so Frannie went out to find him and sure enough there he was; he was having a ride on Dannie's pussy and was laughing like anything.

"I'm having such a lovely rest," he said, "that I won't come back in the book."

"Well, I'll tell my mother on you," said Frannie and ran back in the house.

When Mummie heard all this she didn't say a thing. She just took up the goblin book and turned to the empty page, then she reached for her favorite box of crayons and began drawing something there.

When Frannie saw what she was drawing he ran outside to goblin, who had put his purple cap on Pussy's ear and was still laughing like anything. "I'm playing with Pussy," Goblin said, "so I can't come back in the book."

"You don't have to come back," said Frannie. "Mummie is drawing another goblin on the page where you used to be. She's got out her box of crayons."

Goblin stopped laughing at once and got off Pussy's back. "What is the new goblin like?" he asked. "Anything like me?"

"He's better than you," said Frannie.

"What color is his cap?" asked Goblin.

"Yellow," said Frannie.

"I don't care," said Goblin after doing a little thinking.

"It's a lovely yellow cap," said Frannie.

"I *think* I don't care," said Goblin, "but maybe I do." He put his purple cap back on his head. "And are you going to read about that silly new goblin?"

"Of course I am," said Frannie. "My mother can't stand only half a story so I've got to finish it, right to the very end."

"And," said Goblin, "are you going to put him by your bed where you always put me?"

"I'm not sure about that," said Frannie. "I'll have to think it over."

Goblin was thinking it over, too, and while he was thinking he took off his cap and looked at the pretty purple, then he said, "Tell your mother to stop drawing a minute; tell her I'm only out in the garden thinking the whole thing over."

But when Frannie told Mummie all this she still went on drawing. "I can't wait for any goblin to think anything over. I must hear the rest of this story right to the very end. Besides I'm very fond of drawing and find it hard to stop."

Just at that moment—you know what? *In flew the little goblin!* "Frannie, Frannie!" puffed the goblin, "I've finished thinking it over. I'm tired of Pussy and I've had enough rest and I want to come back in the book! Please stop drawing, Mummie."

"It's too hard to stop," Mummie said. "I'm mad on drawing goblins. I haven't finished the cap."

Goblin cried like anything. "I hate that new goblin," he wept.

Frannie picked up the goblin and held him by his face. "Yes, stop drawing, Mummie," he said, "I like this goblin best. This is the one I want in the book, the one with the purple cap Please stop drawing, Mummie."

Mummie tried to stop drawing but found it far too hard.

The crayon went on by itself. "Any goblin," she said, "who wants to come back in this book will have to wear this cap—a marvelous yellow cap—because I never rub anything out."

Goblin stopped crying at once and dried his tiny tears. "I'll wear that yellow cap," he said, "if it doesn't spoil the book."

"No drawing of mine would spoil a book," said Mummie to the goblin.

"Well, I'll wear it, Mummie, when I'm back in the book."

At last Mummie stopped drawing. Frannie put Goblin back on the page and he put on the yellow cap. He looked lovely in it too. It was cleaner than the purple one, now that he came to think of it.

Frannie kept the purple cap for one of Pussy's ears, then he climbed on Mummie's knee again and went on reading the story, right to the very end."

. . .

After a refresher course for teachers in Ohakune we brought home one of the lecturers with us for the weekend, being unwilling to part with any of them—one of the directors at the Education Department, who said to me, "Do me a film strip."

"What for?"

"You'd make a lot of money."

"Money? I don't want money." Sheer metaphor.

"But . . ." We stood together in the school beneath the Pied Piper who was collecting a bit of dust now, and the chalk was fading a bit; also there were clay marks on it where Jacob —no, young Bernard—had thrown clay. "That's the real reason," I said. "I just plain don't want to."

"You should be writing and illustrating children's stories."

"If the Department wants me to do that they can arrange the time and salary. Let them put a shivering artist on a good warm salary."

"But the Department hasn't the work for a full-time artist."

"No. Neither has New Zealand. There's no place for artists in New Zealand."

"No. But you can't expect the Department to pay you just because you want to draw. How many more would like that too?"

"It's all right," illogically. "If the Department ever created a job for me I doubt if I would take it. As soon as art is measured in money—to me anyway—that's the finish. I just like doing what I want to, drawing when and what I want to, life's too short, too fast, to be doing what you don't want to. I'd do a picture for you though."

He looked up at the large wild dusty picture above us with its hundreds of children following the Piper. "Good, very good."

"Is it?"

"Yes."

"I don't know, of course."

"I could walk right into that picture."

"The real distance is from the outside door."

"The chalk won't last though."

"Can't help that, Pan. It's my favorite medium."

February 11 · Although our division is fighting in Italy in the pit of a European winter, I make my room bright and lovely, releasing again the persistent question of what are we doing for the war, but it is forgotten at school. Yesterday I was working in school on my own clay model of Saul while the little ones were doing theirs. The climate was one I thought existed only in the realm of dreaming . . . those dreams I have of me in some bohemian studio on the Left Bank in Paris or over a bowl of wine in Italy, me all sophisticated and that, with dozens of lovers, paint everywhere and love and communion and sympathy and all that . . . This softly deeply pulsating warmth of common creativity, all artists absorbed in their separate ideas, including my violent self, black heads down to it everywhere and golden ones too, even Pearly and Jacob—this was it materialized, just dropped from the blues of heaven. I *was*—with these naughty children—on the Left Bank of Paris; I *was* in Italy.

On the easel was my guiding sketch of Saul, on the school table my clay, on their desks was their clay and never did better modeling come from the strong lithe fingers of the children: dainty leaves, brave canoes, boats, butterflies, magpies, raupo, ducks, Jacob following mine, and Kata fashioning a doll, her blind eyes uplifted. What had happened to our common violence threatening from the undermind? Perhaps it was escaping by another route.

Paris, Italy and the bowl of wine had all come here.

February 29 · The shining feature of my dreams about Selah to make it a place where I entertain my own kind doesn't shine in reality. My dream didn't allow for glamorous visitors upsetting our uncomfortable unbalance of emotions. Here was another wrecker of unbalances in Selah last weekend, the place where things are not supposed to happen, representing all I longed for in a visitor, even though from the Education Department. Nor did he arrive walking elegantly across the paddock to see me, his hair brushed respectfully; the two of us didn't even walk up the road but ran barefoot across the hills swooping down the gulleys and jumping over thistles. It was Pan, the pleasure god. "Oh," the conversation went in Selah, "now sum me up. You seem to be up on minds."

He laughed a refusal and played with some soft clay on my table.

"Oh, come on now. You began this, you know. You said I was not logical."

"I wouldn't have you changed one bit."

"There you are! You imply there could be changes."

"I like you just as you are." His hair was all over the place and he wore dark glasses.

"That won't do." I poured water in the little teapot.

He put out the cups and saucers. "It's the artistic temperament. You feel things, then arrange your reasons to suit them. But your good taste will prevent you from committing any major bloomer."

"Major bloomer, did you say?"

"Yes. But your sensibility will save you."

"All right," I said. "I'll do you over."

"Oh no," he laughed. "A logical person builds fact on fact and finally comes to his conclusion. But the artistic person jumps to his conclusion intuitively, with a personal bias, then fits in the reasons afterward."

"I try to be logical. I want to be logical."

"But why change? You'll always be interesting, whatever you say. You'll still be interesting when you're seventy."

"I'm tired of being interesting."

"That's interesting."

Later, sitting on the porch, sharing the glamour of the valley, he said, "A logical person builds up fact on fact, then later there is a flash. The correctness of these flashes is in ratio to the correctness of the facts previously built up. A careful and thorough building up of the facts—then the flash."

I didn't answer.

"Your graph," he continued, drawing a zigzag in the air, "is like this: up, down; up, down. A logical person is like this," a smooth horizontal line before him.

"That's how I want to be, like that."

"What? Like Mrs. Blom?"

"Yes. Just like her."

"But you're much more interesting as you are."

"It wears me out."

"Why?"

"Because of the discomfort."

He didn't have an answer to that. I examined the horizon of the ranges. "All my reading is to that end. I read everything of Russell I can understand, hoping that his lovely reasoning, his stunningly clear line of thought . . ."

"Yes, you'd appreciate that."

"It's so symmetrical. 'On the one hand . . . on the other hand . . .' Well, I read him so much hoping that his reasoning will infuse my own. Do you think it might, Pan?"

"No."

"Well, how can I be logical?"

"Stay as you are."

"But it's too uncomfortable."

"Then find the causes of things. Watch for the personal bias."

Heads down together, thoughtful. I said, "I used to be clever."

"You're clever now."

"No, not now—but I used to be. I've gone illogical."

Then Saul arrived, actually walking across the paddock elegantly, his hair brushed respectfully, as I had seen in my dream. "What's going on here?" he said.

Darkness caught the three of us out. Saul had his car but I preferred to walk, Pan and I both preferred to walk. But I was still barefooted though he had shoes, and I couldn't see where to dodge the stones on the road in the now true darkness, at which Pan picked me up and carried me pickaback all the way home through the evening.

March 17 · By now the children are writing and producing, too, their own plays although I don't think it improves their number. This morning first thing Hellen staged her fairy play complete in costume, about which I told her mother later with delighted pride.

"Plays, plays," harshly, "she's full of nothing but her plays at home. I said to her, 'Go and learn something that will be of use to you.' And she said, 'What?' And I said, 'Learn to sew and stop depending on me.' "

"I did teach sewing for two years and your Hellen was the only one who refused to bring either a sugarbag or a flour-bag."

"She won't do a thing for herself," voice rising. "She won't sew the smallest thing."

"Well, I won't teach her to sew. You're a better sewer than I am."

"You can sew!"

"Yes, I can. I made this dress I'm in but I'm not teaching it any more because I just don't like it. I'm prepared to teach other things that people who can sew can't. You can't expect me to be perfect. I'll not teach your Hellen to sew. It's as much as I can do to teach her to come to school on time. You can teach her to sew yourself."

The wretch!

. . .

But it is lovely at school, the soothing discipline and routine, the demands of the children, the chalk and the talk. God be praised for school. Yet this morning I was still remembering that week at New Year and New Year's Day. I suppose I will sometime forget New Year's Day. How I could cry this morning . . . but you can't when there are little ones near you, or when K is about—or when anyone you love is near you. You can't let the darkness inside you diffuse from your eyes to darken others near you. But when K and the children have gone over and Saul is on the step for the milk, "What have you been thinking?" he said.

"About what I'm seeing: proportions, distances, curves." I laid the cloth on the table for lunch.

"Is that what you've been thinking of all the morning?"

"Yes, mostly. Oh, a lot of other things too. I had a little cry this morning, and later a little sing."

"Why did you cry? Why did you cry?"

"Why don't you ask me why I sang?"

"Why did you cry?" He held my shoulders to make me look at him.

"Because I like it."

"Do you always cry in the morning?"

"No. But I did this morning."

"Do you love me?" He picked me up and sat me on the bench.

"Yes."

"Are you telling lies?"

"No."

"You do love me?"

"Yes. Is that important?"

"Yes." He took both my hands and crooned, "You love me, you love me, you love me, you love me . . ."

Saul at his best . . . pursuing.

He said, "When are you coming to see me?"

I left it.

       •   •   •

Moving ever closer to K and finding in him a delightful companion. In him is my salvation. I couldn't live without him. Moreover, I didn't know how fond I was of Pan until after he had gone, and I recall when we said goodbye how he fondled and kissed my hand, the appreciation and respect in it. He's well gone now and I don't expect him to write. But he was musical and merry, adaptable and wonderful. His perceptions were immediate and he left Saul right out. He would answer almost before you had finished saying something . . . full of gentleness and love. To a large extent he understood me. This discriminating delicacy come right into my Selah. If there was any fault in him it was his touch. To me his physical touch did not measure up to his other offerings.

. . .

A long full beautiful letter from Pan. I was warmly moved.

Saul said when he came for the milk in the morning, "You are my child. My all. You are my life."

. . .

The Allies are slogging away in Italy. Mr. Snowdon sent word to me through K that he really wants the whare this time. He said he means to house a family in it to work on his land and this is to be *next Sunday*. Now where can I find another Selah, a Selah Two? It's no good having another look at that other haunted whare where the Maoris won't live either, that's in irrevocable disrepair; besides it's still on Mr. Snowdon's land.

Such a lot of land for the sheer pride of ownership which he has left largely unfenced. On my way to Selah a few weeks ago when I met him ambling along on his horse with his *de facto* Maori wife riding beside him he told me, "I've got the lease of all this land on this side of the road and that side too. I'm a landowner now, Mrs. Henderson. I'm a big landowner now." Sheer landlordship.

"So most of the valley now is under your control, Mr. Snowdon."

It must give him something he needs, status I expect, for he does no more with it than graze a few steers. I claim that he never understood his land, or loved it as such, because I am in the position to know that he neither understood nor loved women. His wife left him, and his daughters, and only his son came to see him once in years and that was about money— whereas land is woman, as the Maoris well know in their chants; it is cultivated to make it produce.

May · On Sunday the children and I looked for a new Selah. As my desire draws me nearer home we examined excitedly the slopes near to the house, with a site for a cave in view, but on account of the way voices carry . . . no, it wouldn't do. Finally I decided on a spot in the forested gully across the road from the school, down the hill behind Saul's place, just asking for a cave. It's about fifty to a hundred yards—yes, about that —down below his cottage but completely hidden by trees. All this is true.

. . .

Late in May now. My writing Saturdays have turned into digging Saturdays, everyone's digging Saturdays, and after school too. K and the children join in and, when he can, Saul, though his spade isn't much. Oh, last Saturday morning . . . all that loose shifting soil, the tea and the biscuits on the top of it in the magic afternoon with the sun on the rewa-rewa leaves and the tuis, dozens of them, wondering what will happen next in their most private domain.

No one is living in the haunted whare yet. Ghost trouble, I think. Mine as well as Whistle's and Mai Mai's. The Saturday before the Sunday it was to be taken over, when Saul brought his car to get my things, he drew me into the doom room and said, "I'll meet you again here someday."

"You can meet me here any time," I said. "My own ghost . . . there she is. Can't you see her? By the window there, where I had my table."

"Yes . . . I can see her."

We came back to the studio. I wanted to say goodbye to my Water-Carrier, my birds on the wall, the "My soul there is a country" one and the vulture I made when I was dying of jealousy, and my sophisticated lady—the kind of lady I wanted to be but couldn't ever be—but Saul disapproved.

"You think I'm sentimental," I said.

"That's why I love you."

I put my cups and teapot into the box, then my brush and shovel.

"You know," he said, "that I need you and that you need me. And that we will always."

"I know," I repeated after him, "that you need me and that I need you and that we will always."

Heaving the Dover stove into the boot of the car later, I asked, "Tell me, what form do you propose to take? I mean, in what form do you propose to meet my ghost here in the future?"

He looked out over the swamp, his eyelids flickering in that way of his when he is thinking deeply. "Ghost unto ghost," he said.

"You've got to die first, to become a ghost."

"Yes."

"That's why she's there . . . that ghost you see there where the table was. She died several times."

Tears . . . from the unsentimental Saul. "If ever I know the night of the soul," he said, "I'd come out of it."

"It would take more than your stubbornness to get you out of that."

We'll meet here again some day. Ghost unto ghost.

. . .

Nearly June, not quite. It's not exactly a cave; you simply dig into the hill a great square step. K put up two walls and a half of punga trunks, an iron roof over it and a simply smashing little narrow door on leather hinges. Then into the bank we dug a fireplace. None of us will forget last Saturday morning when two of us were digging the firebox at the bottom, Saul and K, and I was digging the hole for the chimney from the top simultaneously, until the spades met and clicked within. A fireplace. Ever a requisite of a workroom of mine.

• • •

End of May and nearly winter. Must get this done before winter. I go on digging the fireplace by myself now, measuring and modeling it from the one in Saul's drawing room. I carve imitation bricks, a hob, a hearth, and I'm going to paint the whole thing in red ochre. You'll never know other than that it is a bricked-in fireplace like the one I dreamed about in Selah One. Over the top I've already carved a mantelpiece for a clock and such, to the side I'll make a shelf for books . . .

There's no time for writing about school, or home, or . . .

June · This is the beginning of June. Five A.M. Clay—a clay bank—is a marvelous medium, though why I should continuously operate in nondurable media . . . Above the clay mantelpiece in Selah Two I've carved a Buddha from a bronze model of Saul's. Even Saul held his breath when he saw it. He came in the door, stooping his head, and gasped and said nothing—nothing at all. But I know why. He must have been thinking about all my other drawings and carvings on banks about the valley, some of them well eroded, but I can't say it worries me. And about the chalk drawings on the wall in the whare . . . it would be terrible if they lasted—really!

• • •

June 6 · Finished! I'm terribly happy about Selah Two! D Day today in Europe, but C Day here. Cave Day. We had a cave-warming party this morning, just K and I and Saul and the children. Lyrical! Nobody else knew about it. Lager, bottles and bottles of it.

A cave no more . . . ah, my castle. Some day decades hence, when I'm sitting in some posh studio all lined and that, carpets and curtains and built-in heating, I'll look back to this cave. Sacks on the earthen floor, a small table, no room for a bed, but an old-time armchair picked up from the mart in town, candlelight, a fire and the hum of the rain on the iron. Deep in the jungle of the New Zealand forest a few yards up from a forest stream, thinking aloud endlessly. And the tuis outside on the rewa-rewa . . . you can all but touch them on the intimate trees. And you should see the sun on the rain-wet leaves . . . all this is true.

·   ·   ·

K and I have been working on a track for the children. It leaves the severe little door, winds along the bank of the gully through the trunks, over interesting roots, between flicking ground fern, dipping, dodging, dallying, diving till it rises to the roadside where the blackberry banks. Through which we have cut a tunnel opening secretly on the road itself. At this thorny point, just across the road from the tremendous plum that showers the road with blossom in spring, they pause, examine the road up and down, then dash across to our gate. Pop Vincent himself has not so far discovered this track. My word, do the children use this track, plying to and fro in single file between Mummie and Daddy carrying ridiculous messages. Do the children love this place . . .

July · July, in the middle of winter. Lovely fire, candlelight. Have been digging coal cellar. K and I are very happy, the school and I are, too, but . . . O unhappiness, how everywhere and always you are. Conversation here with Saul today . . . no yesterday . . . sitting in that old armchair. I don't really think he likes this place. His sad face: it is he who is troubled now, at this time. We were talking about a saying to put over my fireplace—not "Nothing matters," for some things do. To know and to be true to oneself.

This place is damp. The winter rains soak the bank. K dug a drain above the cave to turn off the surface water, it does too, but it's still damp, and when I stoke up to dry it out the clay is inclined to crack. I've had a touch of rheumatism lately in my left hip, and I limp when I go to school and it's sore when I wake in the morning—stiff. Lets up a bit later on.

Saul told me last night how much he wanted a woman fully, and to give him children. He claimed my love left him unsatisfied—which of course it has to. He said, "I want a woman. I want a woman very much. I want to love all night every night."

"You'll marry."

"I'll never marry as long as I know you."

I thought of the selection on the River—all impossible. Where can I find a woman for Saul? Here is someone I love wanting something . . .

.   .   .

Sunday evening in spring. I've been writing my novel *Rangatira* for hours: head down over my paper in the evening with the candlelight shaping shadows, thinking to the silence of the night forest noises and feeling absolutely myself. Absolutely free, completely pure . . .

I have some hopes these days of becoming a worthwhile person, studying to that purpose like mad. Sorting myself out as you must in the thirties. I'll pick up all my books now and take them home, it's too damp down here for books. I'll have a hot bath for this hip. I'll not call in at Saul's as I pass it stealthily in the darkness where I'll see the light on in the surgery. He puts on the light in there when he knows I'm still down here, but a doctor should know that it's hard climbing a hill with a hip like mine.

·VIII·

April, 1945 · More than half a year since I put down anything here. When things happen you don't get them down. There's no time. These last years on the River have been an allegro in the symphony of my life, following the andante of the Coast.

I'm working here on a Saturday morning in autumn, the cave softly reminiscent. A little straight line of sun points in through my narrow door touching my head and hands and bringing to life the carved clay Buddha above the fireplace. Through the door the leaves of the forest trees glisten from the last rains and the voices of the tuis ring above the obbligato of the stream, all of it infusing and informing my receptive soul and my overreceptive body which tingles and sparkles with life and love, glistens like the leaves out there; I receive the obbligato of the stream and the bird soprano. I am part of the forest, the New Zealand forest . . . one of its wild creatures.

I've got this strong feeling that this allegro is coming to a close. That the River period is coming to a close. I can read it in K's unspecified excitement, a kind of professional restlessness when a teacher is ready for a change. Teachers don't stay too long in a place if they can help it. I see him studying the gazettes for jobs, waiting for something that is just for him.

Down the bank round the corner from the cave, no more than a few paces, the children have carved out another cave for themselves. No roof or anything, or walls, no more than a seat in the bank. "It's the thinking place," Frannie said, and there they sit on occasion, at peace, gazing among the trunks before them, and down upon the stream, getting their thinking done. I saw Frannie there this morning in wonderful oneness with the forest, a smile on his beautiful face, his hands together, one knee over the other like a philosopher.

"I saw a stranger yestere'en," I wrote to Pan this week, from an ancient rune,
"I put food in the eating place,
Drink in the drinking place,
Music in the listening place,
And in the sacred name of the Triune
He blessed myself and my house."
There should be another line to it:
"We put a seat in the thinking place."
Dear Dannie even wrote on the clay seat, "Thinking Place." In the cave here is the Writing Place. The school is the Teaching Place and the whole valley for the last few years has been the grand Loving Place. A further line to that rune for Pan— "I put kisses in the loving place." But, both being married, we stopped at four. Mind you, they were good ones.

· · ·

Saul the sensitive senses our restlessness. His behavior shows that he does. Sitting in the school when the children had gone for my clay model of him he said, "How long is this going on?"

"Oh, a long time. I don't want to finish at all."

"Well, I'm sick of it, and I'm not going to sit any more."

I was struck.

He went on, "It's too much after a day's work. Too tiring."

"This is the first time you have sat for me after a day's

work. You sat on Saturday and that was the first time for a week."

"The time!" he exclaimed. "You don't notice how the *time* goes by!"

"I appreciate very much the giving of your time. I know how important it is."

"I'll give you," he said, "an hour on Wednesday and an hour on Saturday. And an hour on Sunday. And no more."

The blow landed in the guts. Right at my art . . . as his blow at my music had done, practically winding it. He said he was sick of it. I never forgive attacks on my work. Sick of it . . . It flayed me, scoured me, flagellated. It did more than that.

* * *

Those nightmares I used to have about thrashing the children—they've evaporated long since in the warm normal pulsating of the creative work at school, but where Saul is concerned they haven't. In the evening when I had put the little ones to bed, when they'd finished calling out, wanting a drink or a story, a kiss (or a song) . . . I went over to the school and took up the pointer, a decent firm stick, and went down to the cottage. No light in the drawing room, none in the kitchen, so I went up the corridor to the surgery where he was standing at the high desk, his back to me, writing in his TB records. Just the right position. So I thrashed him. After one glance at me over his shoulder, he went on with his records and I went on thrashing. Shoulders, back, bottom, legs, then the sequence again until there was nothing left of the stick but chips about the floor. Only at one stage had he spoken, at about the third round. "Don't, Sylvia," irritated, "that hurts." Then I went. I stumbled down the hill in the darkness to get over it and sat there in the cave not lighting the candle. But Saul couldn't go on his rounds for a week and showed me the black and blue and brown bruises, ever so proud of them. "Look, I've been to the war," he said.

. . .

One evening in the cave I said, "You hurt me very much when you said you were sick of it."

Surprised, concerned, "Well, I'm . . ."

"Don't say you're sorry." I closed the little door against the forest damp.

"I will say I'm sorry. I wouldn't hurt you for anything. I shouldn't have said it."

"Yes, you should. You should say what you feel. Now I know."

"But I didn't mean it. I just love sitting up there in the school. That was the only day I've found it irksome. I shouldn't have gone that day. I was too tired and irritable."

"It's all right. I don't need you now anyway. I can remember the places."

"I'm going to sit for you tomorrow."

"I don't need you."

"You do. I'll be there at five whether you need me or not."

"I'm not sculpting tomorrow."

"Oh, you wouldn't be, the only day I can come."

"I won't be needing you for a long time. I can remember now."

"I feel very sorry."

"You should feel glad that I'm telling you now and not brooding over it for days."

But I haven't got over it and I feel like crying whenever I think of it.

K said, "And do you mean to say that you're not going to have him sit again?"

"No. I mean I won't *ask* him. I'll use the opportunity if he comes under his own power."

.   .   .

April this is . . . still. It's happened!

About noon—this is Saturday—K came running from the school across the tennis court with a telegram in his hand. Toby Wallop had brought it up from the Store. He pushed it into my hand, puffing. He was appointed to another school, the large one he had applied for. I read it slowly, spelling out each word to myself to make sure, plunging like a knife to uncover its true meaning, until I said, "We'd better make the tea."

.   .   .

Four-thirty Monday morning. Last night in the cave Saul stretched out in the old armchair, a hand over his eyes, after talking about the new job, until the conversation got back to himself. "Go on," he said, "tell me something about myself."

"You're the most selfish person I ever met."

"Good. You get full marks for that." He is always superbly cool in a crisis, until afterwards, and I was not deceived. "And why do you say that?" he asked.

"Because I think it."

"And why do you think it?"

"Because I have known you for nearly three years. More closely than anyone ever has."

He took it apparently with serene gratitude but shortly afterward went out in the darkness and sat in the Thinking Place while I put the kettle over the coals. But I knew from all sorts of familiar signs that he had gone away to cry. As I got two mugs from the clay shelf I thought, Just like before. Pretends it doesn't hurt, then it does, and he lets fly afterward. So I went out the door myself into the forest evening, with the stream saying nothing on our drama but talking away to itself. Round the corner to the Thinking Place to his shadowy shape in the gloom, and I took his hand and led him back into the most humble candlelight of the cave and the most humble warmth of the fire and sat him again in the armchair, while the clay Buddha was worse than the stream in his utter indifference to us, smiling secretively and placidly to himself about the grand jokes of life. I sat beside him and began to comfort him, stroking his black hair, knowing that whatever happened between us, rows or love, I remained his and he remained mine, that, as he had spoken in the haunted whare, "You know that I need you and that you need me, and we will always."

But soon he began to cry until he broke out into loud weeping and shouted, "Go to your new job! Go! Go away!"

He got up but I held him. But he's far stronger than I am and wrenched himself from me and plunged to the door with loud harsh crying. I followed him along the dark track, feeling my way to where he was crying harshly and wildly in the Thinking Place. Or the Crying Place now. And I stood in the night of the forest a moment listening to him, but remembering that New Year when he had taken Delia to tea; I saw again myself crying against the tank stand in my white shorts, hanging on to the pipes, crying through the empty house, crying at the little gate by the pear tree . . . the wild lonely crying such as this, then falling on the grass, my face in it, my fingers tearing it out. "There's *your* pain, you devil!" I cried.

He began pushing down through the jungle of the undergrowth and I remembered all his moments of abandonment when he renounced responsibility; when he had let a patient read the correspondence in the surgery. "I don't care," he had said. "She can read it." And the time when he was amused at my sons climbing along the piping between the tank and the house with the concrete path below them, the time he was minding the children for me, took them to the river and let them play on the boat all the afternoon, times of relapsed responsibility. So I followed him.

From the utter blackness, to the accompaniment of crashing and breaking branches I heard him shouting, "I don't care what happens to me! I'll kill myself!"

So he would if he could. I crashed down after him. "Come back!" I shouted, "come back! You belong to me!"

I heard the fall in the water, then I was there beside him, relieved as he lay prone but his face clear of the water, sobbing distractedly. Sharply I said, "You know I love you."

The crying ceased, he rose, and said with amazing serenity, "Come back up again now. I'm sorry I upset you."

Back in the cave in the candlelight with the Buddha still smiling, I told him, "I don't care what you are, selfish or not. All that concerns me is whether you love me, and if you are near to me. I'm a far worse character than you, which largely you know. But it doesn't matter. Only our loving each other matters."

He took the tea I gave him, but put it down and put his arms round me, weeping softly. So I said again, "I'll never tell you things again like that, I'll never hurt you again. I'll never make you cry again."

"It's good for me."

"It's not good for me though."

. . .

These furious fast years on the River now coming to a close, or rather, coming to another season of the desire to be a worthwhile person. For no one can say I've become that yet or that I'm anywhere nearer. The most I can say is that the desire does endure, which maybe is saying a lot.

Indeed, that any idea whatever should survive what this one has says even more—that in it must be ingredients I did not see at first. A response to exercise like muscles of the body, for a start, and the capacity to increase itself as you see in things that grow. One day, with the season just right, my desire may even fruit in some distant autumn, but that sounds like imagination again galloping off with me—besides, it would take so long. *What* a desire! . . . to live in peace with that word: Myself.

·IX·

Later

Further away again from the center of living. Back on the East Coast, not so far from that other Coast of which I never speak, where we were before the River, but very unlike it. No beaches and tidal rivers but a genuine road.

After the lusciousness of the River valley, the luxury of the forest and flowers, the lavishness of hills and water, we've found ourselves on a burnt white plain that has been a river-bed, not alluvial but based with stones, barely disguised by a half-inch of turf. Manuka does grow in places here but not the cascading white blossom of the River—a species you never saw there. It grows tall and black. Here are these clumps of blackness dramatizing erratically the dry-grass whiteness. On the ear, the only sound the menacing surf of the South Pacific Ocean. The landscape of a nightmare.

. . .

As the taxi carrying us and our little family approached the school residence, a square bare matchbox dropped in the desert, nothing green growing within miles of it, a habitation little more than a shelter from the weather, the first thing my roving eye sought was some kind of Selah Three. Nothing. No Maori whares, haunted or otherwise, no roadman's hut, no army hut, no shed, not even a clump of trees. True, in the distance I saw hills, but out of operative range. Even so I stared that way, examined them as I paused at the gate; without four walls and a roof to call my own, without my regular ration of silence, without my minimum thinking conditions, I could never be a productive person.

In the brilliance of vision that crisis brings I saw what I would do. While the children ran excitedly ahead through the gate and K looked across at the school I saw in mind a small place I would build myself of sods from the ground, enclosed in new-grown trees. I looked down on the ground and dug in a high heel of suede to examine the turf, not only for trees. It clicked on the contour of stones.

I lifted my eyes and surveyed the plain until at a sound other than the sea I gazed into the sky: what I'd heard was the voice of a bird; what I saw was the skim of a skylark. Something alive from the stony earth that was able to rise regardless and sing in the breadth of the blue. "A dare-gale skylark . . . beyond the remembering . . ." After which I went inside.

. . .

April turning to May on the plain. We've been here about three weeks. No longer the old-time school on the hill with only K and me, and our cozy little school roll, but a much larger modern building with rows of stern rooms, a cluster of Maori teachers and hundreds of strange children. Along with my own infant room lapping under seventy I take art and drama throughout the whole school and try to get on with the staff, including a Maori junior.

I don't get the latitude now to indulge in exciting experiment, at least not overtly. Frankly the only circumstance that gets me through the overloaded days, my junior and me, is this very same routine I rejected in the past, so that the two of us revere the timetable. It is our god on the wall. Nevertheless there must be changes. For a start the reading. Still those ridiculous books that I rejected on the Coast and picked up again on the River, being closer beneath the eye of the Department. Department or not, the books *must* relate to the lives of the children, but what to do about it? I'll see.

.   .   .

May and a sudden south wind. Yet the shock of this transition from beauty to bareness, from topographical intimacy to bleak non-intimacy, is a magic catalyst. No longer do I postpone the creative period till after the number and reading but plonk it bang on the morning: for children and lunatics—which covers me—for children and artists, which covers the lot of us, ten o'clock is the peak of the twenty-four hours. Also comparison does its job. Back on the River I seldom recognized that we'd progressed from breaking to making but now I see that we did. Would even Jacob or Pearly, or even young Bernard at the time we left, have systematically and purposefully gouged these holes in the pinex mosaic board?

.   .   .

I'm writing this by the window in the music room on a little table, after the children have gone to bed. A large school, a staff, overflowing infant room and three children of our own at home . . . the need for regular breaths of silence, the wetting of the lips, mouth and throat with the water of silence, is more desperate than before. What about my music, my thinking, my study and my attempt at writing, and the drawing which I loved? What hope of survival for that area within that is the real me? Denying all that, how can I remain sufficiently whole to become a worthwhile person. A worthwhile person must be *all there.*

There's only one thing to do, O my Self. Make yourself a place. The hills are very much too far away to use for a cave and to get there is a mile's walk in full view. I don't like such a distance from home and I never liked "full view." Besides, something these days is moving me to settle nearer home;

whatever I make for myself will be closer than the whare or the cave, closer again to home.

.   .   .

Begin another beginning at school. Destruction had long gone when I left the River, that epic incubator, so had my tongue and my rages in school, yet here they are back again in fullest flood. Talking to those who make and putting out those who break doesn't always work here. Far too many breakers. I'm still puffing from storming at Anzac for throwing a block to smash Sally's house, all done with the devil's smile. The smile I wanted to kill and I did. So lost to passion I was. All with Hiki out of the room of course, training her as I am that neither hand nor voice may be raised in this infant room, certainly not in rage, whenever working with children. There's no need for her to know that I'm not a real teacher but rather a lunatic with wings. As things are now at school it'll be some time before I can return to the gentle sentence I was in the middle of speaking when I left the River school: the sentence about first thing in the morning being the time when we influence others most, when the best of us reaches out to others, whether children, artists, lunatics or larks. Indeed, as I write here now at the school table during the creative work, offering the best of myself to myself, the best of my thinking, such as it is . . . it is first thing in the morning.

Now we clean up—stop.

I heard the mail lorry just then and must go out in a minute to see if there's a letter from Saul, who is halfway to the war . . . the mail once a week again . . . and behind me the lid will lift and Hiki will get out her secret stick she thinks I don't know about. And God knows she might be right.

.   .   .

Winter . . . straight. Senior art this afternoon, about fifty of them; large Maori boys and girls, often bigger than I am and vibrant with pushing sex. Oh, how I miss Hellen and Rosie Tahore—even young Bernard. And I wish I had Kata, those blind eyes flashing up from side to side seeing marvelous things. Acres of color rolling out here, grazing new ideas on the paper, the ideas of Herbert Read. Squares of radiation, interpretative pictures on wide blissful areas: piebald horse, black bank against a sunrise sky; orange clouds, black sea beyond purple hills; trucks in red pouring from heavily laid brushes; white birds, disarming birds upon a turquoise sky . . . why does it stir the tear-dogs, why do I smell freesias when it isn't spring?

I must leave the room a minute to see what's happening to the put-out breakers, then again the lid will lift and the coughing will break out—the epiglottal courting.

· · ·

Nearly spring, and I have taken one of my uncalendared holidays, a professional idiosyncrasy of mine, and Jonquil said tonight, "Oh Mummie, all Standard Three and Four were so disappointed at no drawing yesterday."

"Goodness! They didn't have everything ready, did they?"

"They had all the long easels up and the paper out, and the brushes out and they had all the paint mixed."

"And, dear," from Frannie, "the children wanted dancing today. That's why Adeline had her best dress on today, for dancing today, dear."

To K I said, "I think I might go over each day for drawing and dancing, don't you think?"

"You'd entirely defeat yourself. You're taking a rest so have it."

· · ·

Spring. A spring that is colder than winter. Sod after sod on Wednesday, after seeing it in the paper on Monday, passionately thinking, At least I have life left to love me. Between me and life there is no distance as there is now between me and death. Life is no ghost in Selah One. Even though your steps now will never come to my door in this desert, that doesn't divide life and me. Unlike my ghost conversing with Saul's ghost now in that haunted whare, far-distanced, I can talk to life at will. For I must talk to someone every day outside the heart of my family who are a part of myself, and it is life who answers me. Rising with the skylark from the lonely ground to that place in the blue while two ghosts whisper to each other in that Selah on the river . . . that's where I talk with life.

Sod on sod rising, "Here I am, life, as you made me, to change if you wish, or leave me how you made me . . ." Oh what a place, my life. Yet you have left it, Saul . . .

. . .

Our second spring on the plain after the second winter. Spring on the dappled plain with kowhai in bloom on the hills. I walked with the children there on Sunday. A Friday with a week of school behind me.

Fancy working at Selah with the window and door open and no fire either, after all those freezy drafty months. The larks. That's all I've got for friends—the larks. The flowers in the grass and the hills in the distance. Coming down the track today worn by my own feet, through the long rows of trees we planted . . . for one to stand like that in the spring. Dead. It makes me think of Hopkins' poem about death marking things in the spring, presumably for future reference:

> How cruel a thing
> To mark them in the spring.

I'm trying to work today but fear I have nothing to say . . . having far too much. Often like that.

The weather is warm and I've been carrying water in a

bucket to what's left of the trees—there's a real honeysuckle at the base of Selah sure to be marked by death in the spring.

Or marked . . . as I am . . . by life in the spring.

. . .

Our third spring on the plain. Spring on the plain is different from spring on the River.

This morning I came walking across the sunny paddock with the cruel south wind strangely gone, and as I approached the gate I saw one big girl nudge another big girl and I knew they were thinking of drawing and dancing. Near the school I did an entirely new thing. Was it because of the unexpected dry beauty of the morning, the meadow-down, the "silk-sack clouds," the kowhai in bloom on the hills, the lark enjoying his free occupation underneath the sky? Was it the humility of the adagio at the piano this morning after the bitter prestos of the past two years or the new dazzle I had found on the sour plain?

I took the hand of a child. It was soft, pliant; yielding yet electric. Less tentatively I began to hold it, then more firmly. Another linked on, in their funny way, then another two. They looked up at me in amazed awareness, I down on them in incredulous recognition. Wending our way through the children-crowd before the long stern building, I noticed the teachers staring.

. . .

"M's Hen'son, Peter tol' Davey to give Polly a hideen."

"Go and make something."

From Ani, "Tame broked my house."

"Tame, come here. You broke Ani's house."

"No, I helping the house for Tipu."

No conscious destruction there, not intentional.

"M's Hen'son, Eru droppeen blocks. Broked my peoples."

"Hiki, put him out."

Two years ago an Eru dropped atomic blocks and broked a lot of peoples. To illustrate power and make his point he could have dropped them some place other than on a population. I would have told Hiki, "Put him out."

To deal with the violence in others, one needs first to deal with one's own. I have found there is violence in us all in the jungle of the undermind, in nations as well as in a person. I wouldn't mind getting hold of some people back in my infant room to talk to the makers and put out the breakers. If any of these children—excluding the fools—grow up wanting to kill, then that is my personal failure.

· · ·

You don't hear too much of my tongue these days. The tone improves in the infant room, if you can take the word of a headmaster who is also my husband—not spectacularly with so very many, but visible now and again. I can tell by my own behavior, but then I've been through a very hard school.

Self-forgetfulness in creativity can lead to self-transcendence, which solves many a problem here. At this hour in the morning as I write at this table, everyone is making—except the two fools, Jim and Kuti: what can you do with a fool but avoid him?—for the breakers were put out. I think I might know now, with the World War over, what this work has to do with war.

Some day I'll be a teacher.